Design Patterns and Best Practices in Java

A comprehensive guide to building smart and reusable code in Java

Kamalmeet Singh
Adrian Ianculescu
Lucian-Paul Torje

BIRMINGHAM - MUMBAI

Design Patterns and Best Practices in Java

Commissioning Editor: Kunal Parikh
Acquisition Editor: Alok Dhuri
Content Development Editor: Nikhil Borkar
Technical Editor: Jash Bavishi
Copy Editor: Safis Editing
Project Coordinator: Ulhas Kambali
Proofreader: Safis Editing
Indexer: Rekha Nair
Graphics: Tania Dutta
Production Coordinator: Arvindkumar Gupta

First published: June 2018

Production reference: 1250618

Published by Packt Publishing Ltd.
Livery Place
35 Livery Street
Birmingham
B3 2PB, UK.

ISBN 978-1-78646-359-3

www.packtpub.com

`mapt.io`

Mapt is an online digital library that gives you full access to over 5,000 books and videos, as well as industry leading tools to help you plan your personal development and advance your career. For more information, please visit our website.

Why subscribe?

- Spend less time learning and more time coding with practical eBooks and Videos from over 4,000 industry professionals

- Improve your learning with Skill Plans built especially for you

- Get a free eBook or video every month

- Mapt is fully searchable

- Copy and paste, print, and bookmark content

PacktPub.com

Did you know that Packt offers eBook versions of every book published, with PDF and ePub files available? You can upgrade to the eBook version at `www.PacktPub.com` and as a print book customer, you are entitled to a discount on the eBook copy. Get in touch with us at `service@packtpub.com` for more details.

At `www.PacktPub.com`, you can also read a collection of free technical articles, sign up for a range of free newsletters, and receive exclusive discounts and offers on Packt books and eBooks.

About the authors

Kamalmeet Singh got his first taste of programming at the age of 15, and he immediately fell in love with it. After getting his bachelor's degree in information technology, he joined a start-up, and his love for Java programming grew further. After spending over 13 years in the IT industry and working in different companies, countries, and domains, Kamal has matured into an ace developer and a technical architect. The technologies he works with include cloud computing, machine learning, augmented reality, serverless applications, microservices, and more, but his first love is still Java.

> *I would like to thank my wife, Gundeep, who always encourages me to take up new challenges and brings out the best in me.*

Adrian Ianculescu is a software developer with 20 years of programming experience, of which 12 years were in Java, starting with C++, then working with C#, and moving naturally to Java. Working in teams ranging from 2 to 40, he realized that making software is not only about writing code, and became interested in software design and architecture, in different methodologies and frameworks. After living the corporate life for a while, he started to work as a freelancer and entrepreneur, following his childhood passion to make games.

Lucian-Paul Torje is an aspiring software craftsman who has been working in the software industry for almost 15 years. He is interested in almost anything that has to do with technology. This is why he has worked with everything from MS-DOS TSR to microservices, from Atmel microcontrollers to Android, iOS, and Chromebooks, from C/C++ to Java, and from Oracle to MongoDB. Whenever someone is needed to use new and innovative approaches to solve a problem, he is keen to give it a go!

About the reviewer

Aristides Villarreal Bravo is a Java developer, a member of the NetBeans Dream Team, and a Java User Groups leader. He lives in Panama. He has organized and participated in various conferences and seminars related to Java, JavaEE, NetBeans, the NetBeans platform, free software, and mobile devices. He is the author of jmoordb and tutorials and blogs about Java, NetBeans, and web development.

Aristides has participated in several interviews on sites about topics such as NetBeans, NetBeans DZone, and JavaHispano. He is a developer of plugins for NetBeans.

My m0ther, father, and all family and friends.

Packt is searching for authors like you

If you're interested in becoming an author for Packt, please visit `authors.packtpub.com` and apply today. We have worked with thousands of developers and tech professionals, just like you, to help them share their insight with the global tech community. You can make a general application, apply for a specific hot topic that we are recruiting an author for, or submit your own idea.

Table of Contents

Preface   1

Chapter 1: From Object-Oriented to Functional Programming   5
  Java – an introduction   5
  Java programming paradigms   6
  Imperative programming   6
    Real-life imperative example   6
  Object-oriented paradigm   7
    Objects and classes   7
    Encapsulation   7
    Abstraction   8
    Inheritance   8
    Polymorphism   9
  Declarative programming   10
  Functional programming   11
    Working with collections versus working with streams   11
  An introduction to Unified Modeling Language   12
    Class relations   14
      Generalization   15
      Realization   15
      Dependency   16
      Association   16
        Aggregation   16
        Composition   17
  Design patterns and principles   17
    Single responsibility principle   18
    Open/closed principle   20
    Liskov Substitution Principle   20
    Interface Segregation Principle   22
    Dependency inversion principle   23
  Summary   24

Chapter 2: Creational Patterns   27
  Singleton pattern   27
    Synchronized singletons   29
    Synchronized singleton with double-checked locking mechanism   30
    Lock-free thread-safe singleton   30
    Early and lazy loading   31
  The factory pattern   31
    Simple factory pattern   32

        Static factory   33

        Simple factory with class registration using reflection   34

        Simple factory with class registration using Product.newInstance   35

      Factory method pattern   36

        Anonymous concrete factory   38

      Abstract factory   38

      Simple factory versus factory method versus abstract factory   40

    Builder pattern   40

      Car builder example   41

      Simplified builder pattern   43

      Anonymous builders with method chaining   44

    Prototype pattern   45

      Shallow clone versus deep clone   46

    Object pool pattern   46

    Summary   48

Chapter 3: Behavioral Patterns   49

    The chain-of-responsibility pattern   49

      Intent   50

      Implementation   50

      Applicability and examples   52

    The command pattern   53

      Intent   53

      Implementation   53

      Applicability and examples   55

    The interpreter pattern   56

      Intent   56

      Implementation   57

      Applicability and examples   60

    The iterator pattern   61

      Intent   61

      Implementation   61

      Applicability and examples   63

    The observer pattern   64

      Intent   64

      Implementation   64

    The mediator pattern   65

      Intent   66

      Implementation   66

      Applicability and examples   66

    The memento pattern   67

      Intent   67

      Implementation   67

      Applicability   69

    The state pattern   70

The strategy pattern   70
     Intent   70
     Implementation   71
The template method pattern   71
     Intent   72
     Implementation   72
The null object pattern   72
     Implementation   73
The visitor pattern   73
     Intent   74
     Implementation   74
Summary   75

Chapter 4: Structural Patterns   77
     Adapter pattern   78
         Intent   78
         Implementation   79
         Examples   79
     Proxy pattern   84
         Intent   85
         Implementation   85
         Examples   86
     Decorator pattern   88
         Intent   89
         Implementation   89
         Examples   90
     Bridge pattern   91
         Intent   92
         Implementation   92
         Examples   93
     Composite pattern   95
         Intent   95
         Implementation   96
         Examples   97
     Façade pattern   99
         Intent   99
         Implementation   100
         Examples   101
     Flyweight pattern   103
         Intent   104
         Implementation   104
         Examples   105
     Summary   109

Chapter 5: Functional Patterns   111

Introducing functional programming   111
    Lambda expressions   113
    Pure functions   114
    Referential transparency   114
    First-class functions   114
    Higher-order functions   115
    Composition   115
    Currying   116
    Closure   116
    Immutability   117
    Functors   117
    Applicatives   118
    Monads   119
Introducing functional programming in Java   119
    Lambda expressions   120
    Streams   121
    Stream creator operations   122
    Stream intermediate operations   122
    Stream terminal operations   125
Re-implementing OOP design patterns   125
    Singleton   125
    Builder   126
    Adapter   127
    Decorator   127
    Chain of responsibility   128
    Command   128
    Interpreter   128
    Iterator   129
    Observer   129
    Strategy   130
    Template method   130
Functional design patterns   131
    MapReduce   131
      Intent   131
      Examples   131
    Loan pattern   132
      Intent   132
      Examples   133
    Tail call optimization   133
      Intent   133
      Examples   134
    Memoization   134
      Intent   134
      Examples   135
    The execute around method   136
      Intent   136

Examples	136
Summary	137
Chapter 6: Let's Get Reactive	**139**
What is reactive programming?	139
Introduction to RxJava	141
Installing the RxJava framework	142
Maven installation	142
JShell installation	143
Observables, Flowables, Observers, and Subscriptions	144
Creating Observables	145
The create operator	146
The defer operator	146
The empty operator	147
The from operator	147
The interval operator	148
The timer operator	148
The range operator	148
The repeat operator	149
Transforming Observables	149
The subscribe operator	149
The buffer operator	150
The flatMap operator	150
The groupBy operator	152
The map operator	153
The scan operator	153
The window operator	153
Filtering Observables	154
The debounce operator	154
The distinct operator	154
The elementAt operator	155
The filter operator	155
The first/last operator	156
The sample operator	156
The skip operator	157
The take operator	157
Combining Observables	158
The combine operator	158
The join operator	159
The merge operator	160
The zip operator	160
Error handling	161
The catch operator	161
The do operator	162
The using operator	163

The retry operator   163
Schedulers   164
Subjects   166
Example project   166
Summary   170
Chapter 7: Reactive Design Patterns   171
Patterns for responsiveness   171
Request-response pattern   171
Asynchronous-communication pattern   178
Caching pattern   180
Fan-out and quickest-reply pattern   182
Fail-fast pattern   182
Patterns for resilience   183
The circuit-breaker pattern   183
Failure-handling pattern   184
Bounded-queue pattern   184
Monitoring patterns   185
Bulkhead pattern   185
Patterns for elasticity   186
Single responsibility pattern   186
Stateless-services pattern   188
Autoscaling pattern   190
Self-containment pattern   191
Patterns for message-driven implementation   191
Event-driven communication pattern   191
Publisher-subscriber pattern   192
Idempotency pattern   193
Summary   193
Chapter 8: Trends in Application Architecture   195
What is application architecture?   196
Layered architecture   196
Layered architecture with an example   199
Tiers versus layers   203
What does layered architecture guarantee?   203
What are the challenges with layered architecture?   203
Model View Controller architecture   204
MVC architecture with an example   207
A more contemporary MVC implementation   210
What does MVC architecture guarantee?   210
What are the challenges with MVC architecture?   211
Service-oriented architecture   211
Service-oriented architecture with an example   212
Web services   213

SOAP versus REST   213
Enterprise service bus   214
What does service-oriented architecture guarantee?   216
What are the challenges with service-oriented architecture?   216
Microservices-based Architecture   217
Microservice architecture with an example   217
Communicating among services   219
What does microservices-based architecture guarantee?   219
What are challenges with microservices-based architecture?   220
Serverless architecture   220
Serverless architecture with an example   221
Independence from infrastructure planning   226
What does serverless architecture guarantee?   227
What are the challenges with serverless architecture?   228
Summary   228
Chapter 9: Best Practices in Java   229
A brief history of Java   229
Features of Java 5   230
Features of Java 8   231
Currently supported versions of Java   232
Best practices and new features of Java 9   232
Java platform module system   232
JShell   236
Private methods in interfaces   239
Enhancements in streams   240
Creating immutable collections   241
Method addition in arrays   242
Additions to the Optional class   243
New HTTP client   244
Some more additions to Java 9   245
Best practices and new features of Java 10   247
Local variable type inference   247
copyOf method for collections   249
Parallelization of full garbage collection   250
Some more additions to Java 10   251
What should be expected in Java 11?   252
Summary   253
Other Books You May Enjoy   255
Index   259

Preface

Having knowledge of design patterns enables you as a developer to improve your code base, promote code reuse, and make the architecture more robust. As languages evolve, it takes time for new features to be fully understood before they are adopted en masse. The mission of this book is to ease the adoption of the latest trends and provide good practices for programmers.

Who this book is for

This book is for every Java developer who wants to write quality code. This book talks about a lot of best practices that quite often are missed by developers while coding. The book also covers many design patterns. Design patterns are nothing but best practices to solve particular problems that have been tried and tested by a developer community.

What this book covers

Chapter 1, *From Object-Oriented to Functional Programming*, gives an introduction to different programming paradigms associated with the Java language.

Chapter 2, *Creational Patterns*, introduces the first in a series of design patterns; that is, creational patterns. The chapter talks about various creational design patterns.

Chapter 3, *Behavioral Patterns*, talks about behavioral design patterns. It explains various design patterns to manage behavior of code and objects.

Chapter 4, *Structural Patterns*, introduces you to structural design patterns and explains various widely used design patterns to manage the structuring of objects.

Chapter 5, *Functional Patterns*, introduces readers to functional programming and patterns associated with it.

Chapter 6, *Let's Get Reactive*, introduces you to reactive programming and Java's implementation of it with examples.

Chapter 7, *Reactive Design Patterns*, further explores the pillars of reactive programming and design patterns associated with these pillars.

Chapter 8, *Trends in Application Architecture – from MVC to Microservices and Serverless Applications*, explores architectural patterns that have been tried and tested by developers over the years.

Chapter 9, *Best Practices in Java*, introduces us to the history of Java, best practices, and updates available in the latest versions of Java, and, finally, what is expected in future from Java.

To get the most out of this book

Readers with prior Java experience will be able to gain the most from this book. It is recommended that readers try to explore and play around with the code examples provided in various chapters.

Download the example code files

You can download the example code files for this book from your account at www.packtpub.com. If you purchased this book elsewhere, you can visit www.packtpub.com/support and register to have the files emailed directly to you.

You can download the code files by following these steps:

1. Log in or register at www.packtpub.com.
2. Select the **SUPPORT** tab.
3. Click on **Code Downloads & Errata**.
4. Enter the name of the book in the **Search** box and follow the onscreen instructions.

Once the file is downloaded, please make sure that you unzip or extract the folder using the latest version of:

- WinRAR/7-Zip for Windows
- Zipeg/iZip/UnRarX for Mac
- 7-Zip/PeaZip for Linux

The code bundle for the book is also hosted on GitHub at `https://github.com/PacktPublishing/Design-Patterns-and-Best-Practices-in-Java`. In case there's an update to the code, it will be updated on the existing GitHub repository.

We also have other code bundles from our rich catalog of books and videos available at `https://github.com/PacktPublishing/`. Check them out!

Download the color images

We also provide a PDF file that has color images of the screenshots/diagrams used in this book. You can download it from `http://www.packtpub.com/sites/default/files/downloads/PatternsandBestPracticesinJava_ColorImages.pdf`.

Conventions used

There are a number of text conventions used throughout this book.

`CodeInText`: Indicates code words in text, database table names, folder names, filenames, file extensions, pathnames, dummy URLs, user input, and Twitter handles. Here is an example: "Make the `getInstance` method thread-safe by adding the `synchronized` keyword to its declaration."

A block of code is set as follows:

```
public class Car extends Vehicle
{
  public Car(String name)
  {
    super(name)
  }
}
```

Any command-line input or output is written as follows:

```
java --list-modules
```

Bold: Indicates a new term, an important word, or words that you see onscreen. For example, words in menus or dialog boxes appear in the text like this. Here is an example: "Before this change, you would need the complete **Java Runtime Environment** (JRE) as a whole to be loaded on a server or a machine to run the Java application."

Warnings or important notes appear like this.

 Tips and tricks appear like this.

Get in touch

Feedback from our readers is always welcome.

General feedback: Email feedback@packtpub.com and mention the book title in the subject of your message. If you have questions about any aspect of this book, please email us at questions@packtpub.com.

Errata: Although we have taken every care to ensure the accuracy of our content, mistakes do happen. If you have found a mistake in this book, we would be grateful if you would report this to us. Please visit www.packtpub.com/submit-errata, selecting your book, clicking on the Errata Submission Form link, and entering the details.

Piracy: If you come across any illegal copies of our works in any form on the Internet, we would be grateful if you would provide us with the location address or website name. Please contact us at copyright@packtpub.com with a link to the material.

If you are interested in becoming an author: If there is a topic that you have expertise in and you are interested in either writing or contributing to a book, please visit authors.packtpub.com.

Reviews

Please leave a review. Once you have read and used this book, why not leave a review on the site that you purchased it from? Potential readers can then see and use your unbiased opinion to make purchase decisions, we at Packt can understand what you think about our products, and our authors can see your feedback on their book. Thank you!

For more information about Packt, please visit packtpub.com.

1
From Object-Oriented to Functional Programming

The objective of this chapter is to introduce the reader to the fundamental concepts of writing robust, maintainable, and extendable code using design patterns and the latest features available in Java. In order to achieve our objective, we will cover the following topics:

- What are programming paradigms?
- Imperative paradigm
- Declarative and functional paradigms
- Object-oriented paradigm
- An overview of Unified Modeling Language
- Object-oriented design principles

Java – an introduction

In 1995, a new programming language was released, inspired by the well-known C++ and the lesser known **Smalltalk**. Java was the name of this new language, and it tried to fix most of the limitations its predecessors had. For example, one important feature of Java that made it popular was write once and run anywhere; that is, you could develop your code on a Windows machine and run it on a Linux or any other machine, all you needed was a JVM. It provided additional features such as garbage collection, which freed up the developer from needing to maintain memory allocation and deallocations; the **Just in Time compiler** (**JIT**) made Java intelligent and fast, and removing features such as pointers made it more secure. All the aforementioned features and the later addition of web support made Java a popular choice among developers. Around 22 years later, in a world where new languages come and disappear in a couple of years, Java version 10 has already been successfully launched and adapted by the community, which says a lot about the success of Java.

Java programming paradigms

What are programming paradigms? Since software development began, there have been different approaches to designing programing languages. For each programming language, we have a set of concepts, principles, and rules. Such a set of concepts, principles, and rules is called a programming paradigm. In theory, languages are considered to fall under one paradigm only, but, in practice, programming paradigms are mostly combined in one language.

In the following section, we will highlight the programming paradigms on which Java programming language is based, along with the major concepts that describe these paradigms. These are imperative, object-oriented, declarative, and functional programming.

Imperative programming

Imperative programming is a programming paradigm in which statements are written to change the state of the program. This concept emerged at the beginning of computing and is very close to the computer's internal structure. The program is a set of instructions that is run on the processing unit, and it changes the state (which is stored as variables in the memory) in an imperative manner. The name *imperative* implies the fact that the instructions that are executed dictate how the program operates.

Most of the most popular programming languages today are based, more or less, on the imperative paradigm. The best example of a mainly imperative language is C.

Real-life imperative example

In order to better understand the concept of the imperative programming paradigm, let's take the following example: you're meeting a friend for a hackathon in your town, but he has no idea how to get there. We'll explain to him how to get there in an imperative way:

1. From the Central Station, take tram 1.
2. Get off the tram at the third station.
3. Walk to the right, toward Sixth Avenue, until you reach the third junction.

Object-oriented paradigm

The object-oriented paradigm is often associated with imperative programming, but, in practice, both functional and object-oriented paradigms can coexist. Java is living proof that supports this collaboration.

In the following section, we will briefly highlight the main object-oriented concepts as they are implemented in the Java language.

Objects and classes

Objects are the main elements of an **object-oriented programming** (**OOP**) language. An object holds both the state and the behavior.

If we think of classes as a template, objects are the implementation of the template. For example, if human is a class that defines the behavior and properties that a human being can have, you and I are objects of this human class, as we have fulfilled all the requirements of being a human. Or, if we think of car as a class, a particular Honda Civic car will be an object of this class. It will fulfill all the properties and behaviors that a car has, such as it has an engine, a steering wheel, headlights, and so on, and it has behaviors of moving forward, moving backward, and so on. We can see how the object-oriented paradigm can relate to the real world. Almost everything in the real world can be thought of in terms of classes and objects, hence it makes OOP effortless and popular.

Object-oriented programming is based on four fundamental principles:

- Encapsulation
- Abstraction
- Inheritance
- Polymorphism (subtyping polymorphism).

Encapsulation

Encapsulation basically means the binding of attributes and behaviors. The idea is to keep the properties and behavior of an object in one place, so that it is easy to maintain and extend. Encapsulation also provides a mechanism to hide unnecessary details from the user. In Java, we can provide access specifiers to methods and attributes to manage what is visible to a user of the class, and what is hidden.

Encapsulation is one of the fundamental principles of object-oriented languages. It helps in the decoupling of different modules. Decoupled modules can be developed and maintained more or less independently. The technique through which decoupled modules/classes/code are changed internally without affecting their external exposed behavior is called code refactoring.

Abstraction

Abstraction is closely related to encapsulation, and, to some extent, it overlaps with it. Briefly, abstraction provides a mechanism that exposes *what an object does* and hides *how the object does what it's supposed to do*.

A real-world example of abstraction is a car. In order to drive a car, we don't really need to know what the car has under the hood, but we need to know the data and behavior it exposes to us. The data is exposed on the car's dashboard, and the behavior is represented by the controls we can use to drive a car.

Inheritance

Inheritance is the ability to base an object or class on another one. There is a parent or base class, which provides the top-level behavior for an entity. Every subclass entity or child class that fulfills the criteria to be a part of the parent class can inherit from the parent class and add additional behavior as required.

Let's take a real-world example. If we think of a Vehicle as a parent class, we know a Vehicle can have certain properties and behaviors. For example, it has an engine, doors, and so on, and behavior-wise it can move. Now all entities that fulfill these criteria—for example, Car, Truck, Bike, and so on—can inherit from Vehicle and add on top of given properties and behavior. In other words, we can say that a Car is a *type of* Vehicle.

Let's see how this will look as code; we will first create a base class named Vehicle. The class has a single constructor, which accepts a String (the vehicle name):

```
public class Vehicle
{
  private Stringname;
  public Vehicle(Stringname)
  {
    this.name=name;
  }
}
```

Now we can create a `Car` class with a constructor. The `Car` class is derived from the `Vehicle` class, so it inherits and can access all the members and methods declared as protected or public in the base class:

```
public class Car extends Vehicle
{
  public Car(String name)
  {
    super(name)
  }
}
```

Polymorphism

In broad terms, polymorphism gives us an option to use the same interface for entities of different types. There are two major types of polymorphism, compile time and runtime. Say you have a `Shape` class that has two area methods. One returns the area of a circle and it accepts single integer; that is, the radius is input and it returns the area. Another method calculates the area of a rectangle and takes two inputs, length and breadth. The compiler can decide, based on the number of arguments in the call, which area method is to be called. This is the compile-time type of polymorphism.

There is a group of techies who consider only runtime polymorphism as real polymorphism. Runtime polymorphism, also sometimes known as subtyping polymorphism, comes into play when a subclass inherits a superclass and overrides its methods. In this case, the compiler cannot decide whether the subclass implementation or superclass implementation will be finally executed, and hence a decision is taken at runtime.

To elaborate, let's take our previous example and add a new method to the vehicle type to print the type and name of the object:

```
public String toString()
{
  return "Vehicle:"+name;
}
```

We override the same method in the derived `Car` class:

```
public String toString()
{
  return "Car:"+name;
}
```

Now we can see subtyping polymorphism in action. We create one `Vehicle` object and one `Car` object. We assign each object to a `Vehicle` variable type because a `Car` is also a `Vehicle`. Then we invoke the `toString` method for each of the objects. For `vehicle1`, which is an instance of the `Vehicle` class, it will invoke the `Vehicle.toString()` class. For `vehicle2`, which is an instance of the `Car` class, the `toString` method of the `Car` class will be invoked:

```
Vehicle vehicle1 = new Vehicle("A Vehicle");
Vehicle vehicle2 = new Car("A Car")
System.out.println(vehicle1.toString());
System.out.println(vehicle2.toString());
```

Declarative programming

Let's go back to the real-life imperative example, where we gave directions to a friend on how to get to a place. When we think in terms of the declarative programming paradigm, instead of telling our friend how to get to the specific location, we can simply give him the address and let him figure out how to get there. In this case, we tell him what to do and we don't really care if he uses a map or a GPS, or if he asks somebody for instructions: *Be at the junction between Fifth Avenue and Ninth Avenue at 9:30 in the morning.*

As opposed to imperative programming, declarative programming is a programming paradigm that specifies what a program should do, without specifying how to do it. Among the purely declarative languages are database query languages, such as SQL and XPath, and regular expressions.

Declarative programming languages are more abstract compared to imperative ones. They don't mimic the hardware structure, and, as a consequence, they don't change the programs' states but transform them to new states, and are closer to mathematical logic.

In general, the programming styles that are not imperative are considered to fall in the declarative category. This is why there are many types of paradigms that fall under the declarative category. In our quest, we will look at the only one that is relevant to the scope of our journey: functional programming.

Functional programming

Functional programming is a sub-paradigm of declarative programming. As opposed to imperative programming, functional programming does not change the internal state of the program.

In imperative programming, the functions can be regarded more as sequences of instructions, routines, or procedures. They not only depend on the state stored in the memory but can also change that state. This way, invoking an imperative function with the same arguments can produce different results depending on the current program's state, and at the same time, the executed function can change the program's variables.

In functional programming terminology, functions are similar to mathematical functions, and the output of a function depends only on its arguments, regardless of the program's state, which, at the same time, remains unaffected by the execution of the function.

Paradoxically, while imperative programming has existed since computers were first created, the basic concepts of functional programming dates back before that. Most functional languages are based on lambda calculus, a formal system of mathematical logic created in the 1930s by mathematician Alonzo Church.

One of the reasons why functional languages become so popular in those days is the fact that they can easily run in parallel environments. This should not be confused with multithreading. The main feature that allows functional languages to run in parallel is the basic principle on which they reside: the functions rely only on the input arguments and not on the program's state. That is, they can be run anywhere, and the results of the multiple parallel executions are then joined and used further.

Working with collections versus working with streams

Everyone working with Java is aware of collections. We use collections in an imperative way: we tell the program how to do what it's supposed to do. Let's take the following example in which we instantiate a collection of 10 integers, from 1 to 10:

```
List<Integer> list = new ArrayList<Integer>();
for (int i = 0; i < 10; i++)
{
  list.add(i);
}
```

Now, we will create another collection in which we will filter in only the odd numbers:

```
List<Integer> odds = new ArrayList<Integer>();
for (int val : list)
{
  if (val % 2 == 0)
  odds.add(val);
}
```

At the end, we want to print the results:

```
for (int val : odds)
{
  System.out.print(val);
}
```

As you can see, we wrote quite a bit of code to perform three basic operations: to create a collection of numbers, to filter the odd numbers, and then to print the results. Of course, we could do all the operations in only one loop, but what if we could do it without using a loop at all? After all, using a loop means we tell the program how to do its task. From Java 8 onwards, we have been able to use streams to do the same things in a single line of code:

```
IntStream
.range(0, 10)
.filter(i -> i % 2 == 0)
.forEach( System.out::print );
```

Streams are defined in the `java.util.stream` package, and are used to manage streams of objects on which functional-style operations can be performed. Streams are the functional correspondent of collections, and provide support for map-reduce operations.

We will further discuss streams and functional programming support in Java in later chapters.

An introduction to Unified Modeling Language

Unified Modeling Language (**UML**) is a modeling language that helps us to represent how the software is structured; how different modules, classes, and objects interact with each other, and what the relations between them are.

UML is frequently used in association with object-oriented design, but it has a much broader scope. However, that is beyond the scope of this book, so, in the next sections, we will highlight the UML features relevant to this book.

In UML, we can define the structure and behavior of a system, and we can visualize the model or parts of it through diagrams. There are two types of diagram:

- Structure diagrams are used to represent the structure of a system. There are many types of structure diagrams, but we are only interested in class diagrams. object, package, and component diagrams are similar to class diagrams.
- Behavior diagrams are used to describe the behavior of a system. Interaction diagrams are a subset of behavior diagrams and are used to describe the flow of control and data among different components of a system. Among the behavior diagrams, the sequence diagram is used extensively in object-oriented design.

Class diagrams are the type of diagrams used most in object-oriented design and development stages. They are a type of structure diagram, and are used to illustrate the structure of classes and the relations among them:

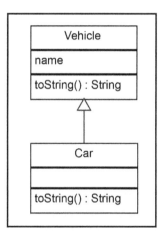

Class diagrams are useful for describing how the classes are structured in an application. Most of the time, just looking at the structure can be enough to be able to understand how the classes interact, but sometimes this is not enough. For those cases, we can use behavior and interaction diagrams, of which the sequence diagram is used to describe class and object interaction. Let's use a sequence diagram to show how the **Car** and **Vehicle** objects interact in the inheritance and polymorphism example:

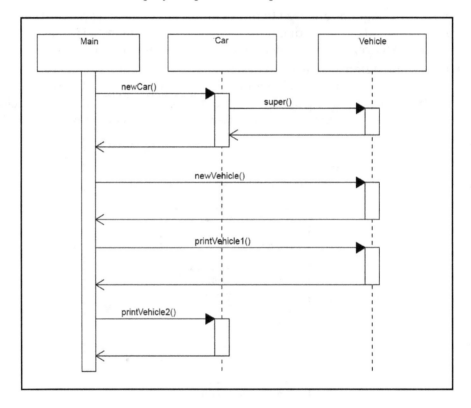

Class relations

In object-oriented programming, besides the inheritance relation that represents one of the fundamental concepts, there are a few other class relations that help us to model and develop complex software systems:

- Generalization and realization
- Dependency
- Association, aggregation, and composition

Generalization

Inheritance is also called an **is-a** relationship because the class inherited from another class can be used as the superclass.

When a class represents the shared characteristics of more than one class, it is called a **generalization**; for example, **Vehicle** is a generalization of **Bike**, **Car**, and **Truck**. Similarly, when a class represents a special instance of a general class, it is called a **specialization**, so a **Car** is a specialization of **Vehicle**, as shown in the following diagram:

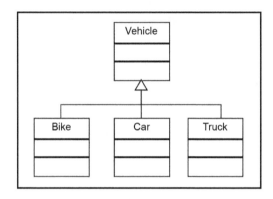

In UML terminology, the relation to describe inheritance is called Generalization.

Realization

If generalization is the corresponding term in UML for object-oriented inheritance, realization, in UML, represents the implementation of an interface by a class in object-oriented programming.

Let's assume we create an interface called **Lockable**, which is implemented only by **Vehicles** that can be locked. In this case, a version of the previous diagram implementing **Lockable** for the **Car** class will look like this:

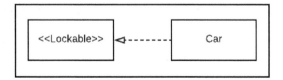

Dependency

Dependency is one of the most generic types of UML relationship. It is used to define that one class depends in some way or other on another class, while the other class may or may not depend on the first one. A dependent relationship is used to represent relations that do not fall into one of the cases described in the following sections. Dependency is sometimes called **Uses-A** relationship.

In general, in object-oriented programming languages dependency is used to describe whether one class contains a parameter of the second class in the signature of a method, or whether it creates instances of the second class by passing them to other classes without using them (without invoking its methods):

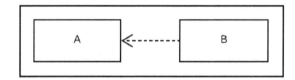

Association

An association represents the relationship between two entities. There are two types of association, namely composition and aggregation. In general, an association is represented by an arrow, as shown in the following diagram:

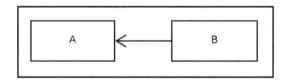

Aggregation

An aggregation is a special type of association. If inheritance is considered to be the is-a relationship, aggregation can be considered to be the **HAS-A** relationship.

Aggregation is used to describe a relation between two or more classes, when one class contains the other from a logical point of view, but instances of the contained class can live independently of the first class, outside of its context, or can be shared among other classes. For example, a **Department** HAS-A **Teacher**; additionally, every **Teacher** must belong to **Department**, but if a **Department** ceases to exist, a **Teacher** can still be active as shown in the following diagram:

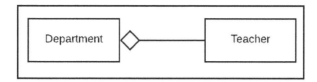

Composition

As the name suggests, a class is a composition of another one. This is somewhat similar to aggregation, with the difference being that the dependent class ceases to exist when the main class ceases to exist. For example, a **House** is made up of a **Room**, but the **Room** ceases to exist if the **House** is destroyed, as shown in the following diagram:

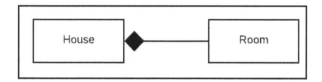

In practice, especially in languages such as Java that have garbage collectors, the boundary between composition and aggregation is not so well defined. Objects are not destroyed manually; when they are no longer referenced, they are automatically destroyed by the garbage collector. For this reason, from a coding point of view, we should not really be concerned if we deal with a composition or an aggregation relationship, but it's important if we want to have a well-defined model in UML.

Design patterns and principles

Software development is a process that is not only about writing code, regardless of whether you are working in a large team or on a one-person project. The way an application is structured has a huge impact on how successful a software application is.

When we are talking about a successful software application, we are not only discussing how the application does what it's supposed to do but also how much effort we put into developing it, and if it's easy to test and maintain. If this is not done in a correct manner, the skyrocketing development cost will result in an application that nobody wants.

Software applications are created to meet needs, which are constantly changing and evolving. A successful application should also provide an easy way through which it can be extended to meet the continuously changing expectations.

Luckily, we are not the first to encounter these problems. Some of the problems have already been faced and handled. These common problems can be avoided or solved if a set of object-oriented design principles and patterns are applied while designing and developing software.

The object-oriented design principles are also called **SOLID**. These principles are a set of rules that can be applied when designing and developing software, in order to create programs that are easy to maintain and develop. They were first introduced by Robert C. Martin, and they are part of the agile software-development process. The SOLID principles include the single responsibility principle, open/closed principle, Liskov Substitution Principle, Interface Segregation Principle, and dependency inversion principle.

In addition to the design principles, there are object-oriented design patterns. Design patterns are general reusable solutions that can be applied to commonly occurring problems. Following Christopher Alexander's concept, design patterns were first applied to programming by Kent Beck and Ward Cunningham, and they were popularized by the so-called **Gang Of Four** (**GOF**) book in 1994. In the following section, we will present the SOLID design principles, which will be followed by the design patterns in the next chapters.

Single responsibility principle

The single responsibility principle is an object-oriented design principle that states that a software module should have only one reason to change. In most cases, when writing Java code, we will apply this to classes.

The single responsibility principle can be regarded as a good practice for making encapsulation work at its best. A reason to change is something that triggers the need to change the code. If a class is subject to more than one reason to change, each of them might introduce changes that affect others. When those changes are managed separately but affect the same module, one set of changes might break the functionality related to the other reasons for change.

On the other hand, each responsibility/reason to change will add new dependencies, making the code less robust and harder to change.

In our example, we will use a database to persist the objects. Let's assume that, for the **Car** class, we will add methods to handle the database operations of create, read, update, and delete, as shown in the following diagram:

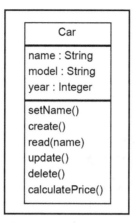

In this case, the **Car** will not only encapsulate the logic, but also the database operations (two responsibilities are two reasons to change). This will make our classes harder to maintain and test, as the code is tightly coupled. The **Car** class will depend on the database, so if in the future we want to change the database system, we have to change the **Car** code. This might generate errors in the **Car** logic.

Conversely, changing the **Car** logic might generate errors in the data persistence.

The solution would create two classes: one to encapsulate the **Car** logic and the other to be responsible for persistence:

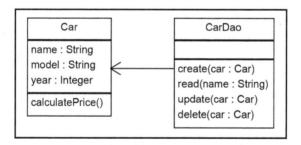

Open/closed principle

This principle is as follows:

> *"Modules, classes, and functions should be open for extension but closed for modifications."*

Applying this principle will help us to develop complex and robust software. We must imagine the software we develop is building a complex structure. Once we finish a part of it, we should not modify it any more but build on top of it.

When developing software, it's the same. Once we have developed and tested a module, if we want to change it, we must test not only the functionality we are changing but the entire functionality it's responsible for. That involves a lot of additional resources, which might not have been estimated from the beginning, and also can bring additional risks. Changes in one module might affect functionality in others or on the whole. The following is a diagrammatic representation:

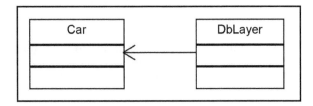

For this reason, best practice is to try to keep modules unchanged once finished and to add new functionality by extending them using inheritance and polymorphism. The open/closed principle is one of the most important design principles being the base for most of the design patterns.

Liskov Substitution Principle

Barbara Liskov states that, *Derived types must be completely substitutable for their base types.* The **Liskov Substitution Principle** (**LSP**) is strongly related to subtyping polymorphism. Based on subtyping polymorphism in an object-oriented language, a derived object can be substituted with its parent type. For example, if we have a `Car` object, it can be used in the code as a `Vehicle`.

Chapter 1

The LSP states that, when designing the modules and classes, we must make sure that the derived types are substitutable from a behavior point of view. When the derived type is substituted with its supertype, the rest of the code will operate with it as it is the subtype. From this point of view, the derived type should behave as its supertype and should not break its behavior. This is called strong behavioral subtyping.

In order to understand the LSP, let's take an example in which the principle is violated. While we are working on the car-service software, we discover we need to model the following scenario. When a car is left for service, the owner leaves the car. The service assistant takes the key and, when the owner leaves, he goes to check that he has the right key and that he has spotted the right car. He simply goes to unlock and lock the car, then he puts the key in a designated place with a note on it so the mechanic can easily pick it up when he has to inspect the car.

We already have defined a `Car` class. We are now creating a `Key` class and adding two methods into the car class: lock and unlock. We add a corresponding method, so the assistant checks the key matches the car:

```
public class Assistant
{
  void checkKey(Car car, Key key)
  {
    if ( car.lock(key) == false ) System.out.println("Alert! Wrong
    key, wrong car or car lock is broken!");
  }
}
```

The diagram is as follows:

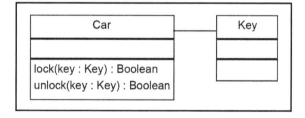

[21]

While working on our software, we realize that buggies are sometimes repaired through the car service. As buggies are four-wheel cars, we create a **Buggy** class, which is inherited from the **Car**:

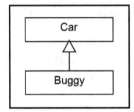

Buggies don't have doors, so they cannot be locked or unlocked. We implement our code accordingly:

```
public bool lock(Key key)
{
    // this is a buggy so it can not be locked return false;
}
```

We design our software to work with cars, regardless of whether they are buggies or not, so in the future we might extend it with other types of cars. A problem may arise from the fact that cars are expected to be locked and unlocked.

Interface Segregation Principle

The following quote is taken from `https://www.oodesign.com/interface-segregation-principle.html` link:

> *"Clients should not be forced to depend upon interfaces that they don't use."*

When applied, the **Interface Segregation Principle (ISP)** reduces the code coupling, making the software more robust, and easier to maintain and extend. ISP was first announced by Robert Martin, when he realized that if the principle is broken and clients are forced to depend on interfaces they don't use, the code becomes so tightly coupled that it's almost impossible to add new functionality to it.

In order to better understand this, let's again take the car-service example (refer to the following diagram). Now we need to implement a class named **Mechanic**. The mechanic repairs cars, so we add a method of repair car. In this case, the **Mechanic** class depends upon the *I* class. However, the **Car** class exposes a richer sets of methods than the **Mechanic** class needs:

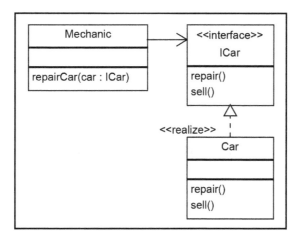

This is a bad design because if we want to replace a car with another one, we need to make changes in the **Mechanic** class, which violates the open/closed principle. Instead, we must create an interface that exposes only the relevant methods required in the **Mechanic** class, as shown in the following diagram:

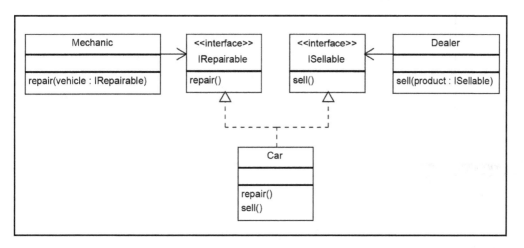

Dependency inversion principle

"High-level modules should not depend on low-level modules. Both should depend on abstractions."

"Abstractions should not depend on details. Details should depend on abstractions."

In order to understand this principle, we must explain the important concept of coupling and decoupling. Coupling refers to the degree to which modules of a software system are dependent on one another. The lower the dependency is, the easier it is to maintain and extend the system.

There are different approaches to decoupling the components of a system. One of them is to separate the high-level logic from the low-level modules, as shown in the following diagram. When doing this, we should try to reduce the dependency between the two by making them depend on abstractions. This way, any of them can be replaced or extended without affecting other modules:

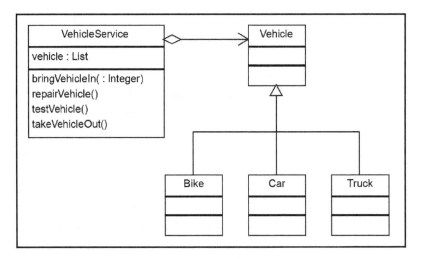

Summary

In this chapter, we presented the main programming paradigms used in Java. We have learned that two different paradigms, such as imperative programming and functional programming, can coexist in the same language; and we have learned how Java went from pure, imperative object-oriented programming to integrating functional programming elements.

Although Java introduced new functional elements, starting from version 8, it is at its core still an object-oriented language. In order to write solid and robust code that is easy to extend and maintain, we learned about the fundamental principles of object-oriented programming languages.

An important part of developing software is designing the structure and the desired behavior of the components of our programs. This way, we can work on large systems, in large teams, sharing our object-oriented designs within or between teams. In order to be able to do this, we highlighted the main UML diagrams and concepts relevant to object-oriented design and programming. We also use UML extensively in our book to describe the examples.

After introducing the class relationships and showing how to represent them in diagrams, we dove into the next section, where we described what the object-oriented design patterns and principles are, and we presented the main principles.

In the next chapter, we will move on to presenting the group of design patterns dealing with object creation in such a way that our code is robust and extendable.

2
Creational Patterns

The objective of this chapter is to learn about creational patterns. Creational patterns are patterns that deal with object creation. In this chapter, we will cover the following topics:

- Singleton pattern
- Simple factory pattern
- Factory method patterns
- Abstract factory pattern
- Builder pattern
- Prototype pattern
- Object pool pattern

Singleton pattern

The singleton pattern is probably the most widely used design pattern since the inception of Java. It is a simple pattern, easy to understand and to use. Sometimes it is used in excess, and in scenarios where it is not required. In such cases, the disadvantages of using it outweigh the advantages it brings. For this reason, the singleton is sometimes considered an anti-pattern. However, there are many scenarios where singletons are necessary.

As its name suggests, the singleton pattern is used to ensure that only a single instance of an object can be created. In addition to that, it also provides global access to that instance. The implementation of a singleton pattern is described in the following class diagram:

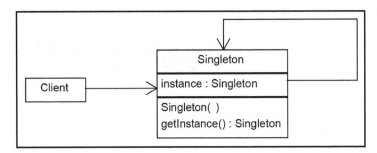

The implementation of the singleton pattern is very simple and consists of a single class. To ensure that the singleton instance is unique, all singleton constructors should be made private. Global access is done through a static method that can be globally accessed to get the singleton instance, as shown in the following code:

```
public class Singleton
{
  private static Singleton instance;
  private Singleton()
  {
    System.out.println("Singleton is Instantiated.");
  }
  public static Singleton getInstance()
  {
    if (instance == null)
    instance = new Singleton();
    return instance;
  }
  public void doSomething()
  {
    System.out.println("Something is Done.");
  }
}
```

When we need to use the singleton object somewhere in our code, we simply invoke it like this:

```
Singleton.getInstance().doSomething();
```

In the `getInstance` method, we check whether the instance is null. If the instance is not null, it means the object was created before; otherwise, we create it using the new operator. After that, in either case, it is not null anymore, so we can return the instance object.

Synchronized singletons

The code for synchronized singletons is simple and efficient, but there is a situation we should take into consideration. If we use our code in a multithreading application, it may be the case that two threads invoke the `getInstance` method at the same time when the instance is null. When this happens, it may be the case that the first thread proceeds to instantiate the singleton using the new operator, and, before finishing it, the second thread checks whether the singleton is null. Since the first thread didn't finish instantiating it, the second thread will find that the instance is null, so it will start instantiating it too.

This scenario may seem almost impossible, but if it takes a long time to instantiate the singleton, the likelihood of it happening is high enough that it cannot be neglected.

The solution to this problem is very simple. We have to make the block that checks whether the instance is null thread-safe. This can be done in the following two ways:

- Making the `getInstance` method thread-safe by adding the `synchronized` keyword to its declaration:

  ```
  public static synchronized Singleton getInstance()
  ```

- Wrapping the `if (instance == null)` condition in a `synchronized` block. When we use the `synchronized` block in this context, we need to specify an object that provides the lock. We use the `Singleton.class` object for this, as shown in the following code snippet:

  ```
  synchronized (SingletonSync2.class)
  {
    if (instance == null)
    instance = new SingletonSync2();
  }
  ```

Synchronized singleton with double-checked locking mechanism

The previous implementation is thread-safe but it introduces an unnecessary delay: the block that checks whether the instance has already been created is synchronized. This means that the block can be executed by only one thread at a time, but locking makes sense only when the instance has not been created. When the singleton instance has already been created, each thread can get the current instance in an unsynchronized manner.

Adding an additional condition before the `synchronized` block will move the thread-safe locking only when the singleton has not been instantiated yet:

```
if (instance == null)
{
  synchronized (SingletonSync2.class)
  {
    if (instance == null)
    instance = new SingletonSync2();
  }
}
```

Note that `instance == null` is checked twice. This is necessary, because we have to make sure a check is done in the `synchronized` block too.

Lock-free thread-safe singleton

One of the best implementations of the singleton pattern in Java relies on the fact that a class is loaded a single time. By instantiating the static member directly when declared, we make sure that we have a single instance of the class. This implementation avoids locking mechanisms and additional checking to see whether the instance has already been created:

```
public class LockFreeSingleton
{
  private static final LockFreeSingleton instance = new
  LockFreeSingleton();
  private LockFreeSingleton()
  {
    System.out.println("Singleton is Instantiated.");
  }
  public static synchronized LockFreeSingleton getInstance()
  {
    return instance;
  }
```

```
public void doSomething()
{
  System.out.println("Something is Done.");
}
}
```

Early and lazy loading

Singletons can be split into two categories, depending on when the instance object is created. If the singleton is created when the application is started, it is considered an **early/eager instantiation**. Otherwise, if the singleton constructor is invoked when the getInstance method is invoked for the first time, it is considered a **lazy-loading singleton**.

The lock-free thread-safe singleton presented in the previous example is considered an early-loading singleton in the first version of Java. However, in the latest version of Java, classes are loaded when they are needed, so that version is also a lazy-loading version. Furthermore, the moment that a class is loaded depends on the JVM implementation and may differ from one version to another. Making design decisions based on JVM implementation should be avoided.

Currently, there is no reliable option in Java for creating an early loading singleton. If we really need an early instantiation, we should enforce it at the start of the application, by simply invoking the getInstance() method, as shown in the following code:

```
Singleton.getInstance();
```

The factory pattern

As discussed in the previous chapter, inheritance is one of the fundamental concepts in object-oriented programming. Along with subtyping polymorphism, it gives us the is/a relationship. A Car object can be handled as a Vehicle object. A Truck object can be handled as a Vehicle object too. On one hand, this kind of abstraction makes our code thinner, because the same piece of code can handle operations for both Car and Truck objects. On the other hand, it gives us the option to extend our code to new types of Vehicle objects by simply adding new classes such as Bike and Van without modifying it.

When we deal with such scenarios, one of the trickiest parts is the creation of objects. In object-oriented programming, each object is instantiated using the constructor of the specific class, as shown in the following code:

```
Vehicle vehicle = new Car();
```

This piece of code implies a dependency between the class which instantiates an object and the class of the instantiated object. Such dependencies make our code tightly coupled and harder to extend without modifying it. For example, if we need to replace Car with another type, let's say Truck, we need to change the code accordingly:

```
Vehicle vehicle = new Truck();
```

But there are two problems here. First of all, our class should be open for extension but closed for modification (the open/closed principle). Second of all, each class should have only one reason to change (the single responsibility principle). Changing the main code each time we add a new class will break the open/closed principle, and having the main class responsible for instantiating vehicle objects in addition to its functionality will break the single responsibility principle.

In this case, we need to come up with a better design for our code. We can add a new class that is responsible for instantiating vehicle objects. We are going to call the pattern based on this SimpleFactory class.

Simple factory pattern

The factory pattern is used to encapsulate the logic to instantiate objects referred through a common interface. New classes can be added with minimal changes.

The implementation of a simple factory is described in the following class diagram:

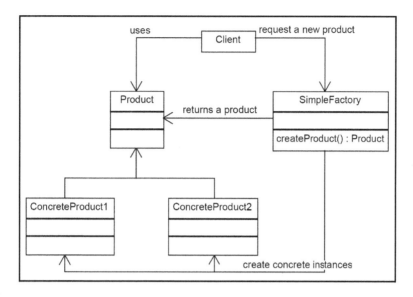

The `SimpleFactory` class implements the code to instantiate `ConcreteProduct1` and `ConcreteProduct2`. When the client needs an object, it calls the `createProduct()` method of the `SimpleFactory` with the parameter indicating the type of object it requires. `SimpleFactory` instantiates the corresponding concrete product and returns it. The returned product is cast to the base class type so the client will handle any `Product` in the same way, regardless of whether it is a `ConcreteProduct1` or `ConcreteProduct2`.

Static factory

Let's write a simple factory to create instances of vehicles. We have an abstract `Vehicle` class and three concrete classes inherited from it: `Bike`, `Car`, and `Truck`. The factory, also called the static factory, will look like this:

```
public class VehicleFactory
{
  public enum VehicleType
  {
    Bike,Car,Truck
  }
  public static Vehicle create(VehicleType type)
  {
    if (type.equals(VehicleType.Bike))
    return new Bike();
    if (type.equals(VehicleType.Car))
    return new Car();
```

```
        if (type.equals(VehicleType.Truck))
        return new Truck();
        else return null;
    }
}
```

The factory looks very simple and is responsible for the instantiation of the `vehicle` classes, complying with the single responsibility principle. It helps us to reduce coupling because the client depends only on the `Vehicle` interface, complying with the dependency inversion principle. If we need to add a new `vehicle` class, we need to change the `VehicleFactory` class, so the open/closed principle is broken.

We can improve the simple factory pattern to make it open for extension but closed for modification by using a mechanism to register new classes that will be instantiated when needed. There are two ways to achieve this:

- Registering product class objects and instantiating them using reflection
- Registering product objects and adding a `newInstance` method to each product that returns a new instance of the same class as itself

Simple factory with class registration using reflection

For this method, we are going to use a map to keep the product IDs along with their corresponding classes:

```
private Map<String, Class> registeredProducts = new
HashMap<String,Class>();
```

Then, we add a method to register new vehicles:

```
public void registerVehicle(String vehicleId, Class vehicleClass)
{
    registeredProducts.put(vehicleId, vehicleClass);
}
```

The `create` method becomes the following:

```
public Vehicle createVehicle(String type) throws InstantiationException,
IllegalAccessException
{
    Class productClass = registeredProducts.get(type);
    return (Vehicle)productClass.newInstance();
}
```

In certain situations, working with reflection is either impossible or discouraged. Reflection requires a runtime permission that may not be present in certain environments. If performance is an issue, reflection may slow the program and so should be avoided.

Simple factory with class registration using Product.newInstance

In the previous code, we used reflection to instantiate new vehicles. If we have to avoid reflection, we can use a similar factory where to register the new vehicle classes the factory should be able to create. Instead of adding classes to the map, we are going to add instances of each type of object we want to register. Each product will be able to create a new instance of itself.

We start by adding an abstract method in the base `Vehicle` class:

```
abstract public Vehicle newInstance();
```

For each product, the method declared abstract in the base class must be implemented:

```
@Override
public Car newInstance()
{
   return new Car();
}
```

In the `factory` class, we are going to change the map to keep the IDs of the objects along with the `vehicle` objects:

```
private Map<String, Vehicle> registeredProducts = new
HashMap<String,Vehicle>();
```

Then we register a new type of vehicle by passing an instance of it:

```
public void registerVehicle(String vehicleId, Vehicle vehicle)
{
   registeredProducts.put(vehicleId, vehicle);
}
```

We change the `createVehicle` method accordingly:

```
public AbstractProduct createVehicle(String vehicleId)
{
   return registeredProducts.get(vehicleId).newInstance();
}
```

Factory method pattern

The factory method pattern is an improvement upon the static factory. The `factory` class is made abstract and the code to instantiate specific products is moved to subclasses that implement an abstract method. This way, the `factory` class can be extended without being modified. The implementation of a factory method pattern is described in the following class diagram:

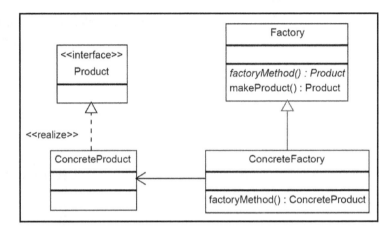

It's time for some example code. Let's assume we have a car factory. At the moment, we produce two car models: a small sports car and a large family car. In our software, the customer can decide whether they want a small car or a large car. To start with, we are creating a `Vehicle` class with two subclasses: `SportCar` and `SedanCar`.

Now that we have the vehicle structure, let's build the abstract factory. Please note that the factory does not have any code to create new instances:

```
public abstract class VehicleFactory
{
  protected abstract Vehicle createVehicle(String item);
  public Vehicle orderVehicle(String size, String color)
  {
    Vehicle vehicle = createVehicle(size);
    vehicle.testVehicle();
    vehicle.setColor(color);
    return vehicle;
  }
}
```

To add the code to create car instances, we subclass the `VehicleFactory`, creating a `CarFactory`. The car factory has to implement the `createVehicle` abstract method, which is invoked from the parent class. Practically, the `VehicleFactory` delegates the concrete vehicle's instantiation to the subclasses:

```
public class CarFactory extends VehicleFactory
{
  @Override
  protected Vehicle createVehicle(String size)
  {
    if (size.equals("small"))
    return new SportCar();
    else if (size.equals("large"))
    return new SedanCar();
    return null;
  }
}
```

In the client, we simply create the factory and create orders:

```
VehicleFactory carFactory = new CarFactory();
carFactory.orderVehicle("large", "blue");
```

At this point, we realize how much profit a car factory can bring. It's time to extend our business, and our market research tells us that there is a high demand for trucks. So let's build a `TruckFactory`:

```
public class TruckFactory extends VehicleFactory
{
  @Override
  protected Vehicle createVehicle(String size)
  {
    if (size.equals("small"))
    return new SmallTruck();
    else if (size.equals("large"))
    return new LargeTruck();
    return null;
  }
}
```

When an order is started, we use the following code:

```
VehicleFactory truckFactory = new TruckFactory();
truckFactory.orderVehicle("large", "blue");
```

Anonymous concrete factory

We continue the previous code by adding a `BikeFactory` from where customers can select a small bike or a large bike. We can do this without creating a separate class file; we can simply create an anonymous class that extends the `VehicleFactory` directly in the client code:

```
VehicleFactory bikeFactory = new VehicleFactory()
{
  @Override
  protected Vehicle createVehicle(String size)
  {
    if (size.equals("small"))
    return new MountainBike();
    else if (size.equals("large"))
    return new CityBike();
    return null;
  }
};
bikeFactory.orderVehicle("large", "blue");
```

Abstract factory

The abstract factory is an extended version of the factory method. Instead of creating a single type of object, it is used to create a family of related objects. If the factory method had one `AbstractProduct`, the abstract factory has several `AbstractProduct` classes.

The factory method has an abstract method that is implemented by each concrete factory with the code to instantiate the abstract product. The abstract factory has one method for each abstract product.

If we take the abstract factory pattern and we apply it to a *family containing a single object*, then we have a factory method pattern. The factory method is just a particular case of the abstract factory.

The implementation of an abstract factory pattern is described in the following class diagram:

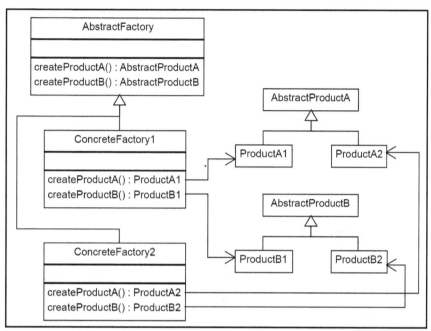

The abstract factory pattern is composed of the following classes:

- AbstractFactory: This is the abstract class that declares the methods that are creating types of products. It contains a method for each AbstractProduct that has to be created.
- ConcreteFactories: Concrete classes that implement the methods declared in the AbstractFactory base class. There is a factory for each set of concrete products.
- AbstractProducts: The base interfaces or classes for objects that are required. A family of related products is made up of similar products from each hierarchy: ProductA1 and ProductB1 are from the first family of classes, which is instantiated by ConcreteFactory1; the second family, ProductA2 and ProductB2, is instantiated by ConcreteFactory2.

Simple factory versus factory method versus abstract factory

We have talked about three ways to implement the factory pattern, namely, the simple factory, the factory method, and the abstract factory pattern. If you are confused about these three implementations, you are not to be blamed, as there is a lot of overlap between them. Moreover, there is no single definition of these patterns, and experts may differ on how they should be implemented.

The idea is to understand the core concept. At its core, we can say that the factory pattern is all about delegating the responsibility for the creation of appropriate objects to a factory class. If our factory is complex, that is, it should serve multiple types of objects or factories, we can modify our code accordingly.

Builder pattern

The builder pattern serves the same purpose as the other creational patterns, but it does so in a different way and for different reasons. When developing complex applications, the code tends to become more complex. Classes tend to encapsulate more functionality and, at the same time, class structures become more complex. As the functionality grows, more scenarios need to be covered and, for these, different representations of classes are required.

When we have a complex class that we need to instantiate to different objects with different structures or different internal states, we can use separate classes to encapsulate the instantiation logic. These classes are called **builders**. Each time we need objects from the same class with a different structure, we can create another builder to create such instances.

The same concept can be used not only for classes for which we need different representations but also for complex objects composed of other objects.

Creating builder classes to encapsulate the logic to instantiate complex objects is consistent with the single responsibility principle and with the open/closed principle. The logic to instantiate a complex object is moved to a separate **Builder** class. When we need objects with different structures, we can add new builder classes, so the code is closed for modification and open for extension, as shown in the diagram:

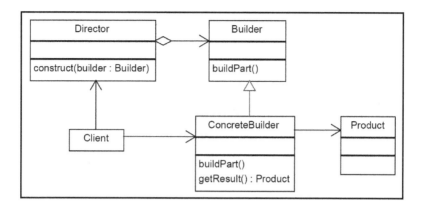

The following classes are involved in the builder pattern:

- `Product`: The class whose objects we have to build. It is a complex or a composite object of which we need different representations.
- `Builder`: The abstract class or interface which declares the parts from which the product is built. Its role is to expose only the functionality required to build the `Product`, hiding the rest of the `Product` functionality; it decouples the `Product` from the higher-level class that builds it.
- `ConcreteBuilder`: A concrete builder that implements the methods declared in the `Builder` interface. In addition to the methods declared in the `Builder` abstract class, it has a `getResult` method that returns the built product.
- `Director`: A class that directs how the object is built. In some variants of the builder pattern this class is removed, its role being taken by either the client or the builder.

Car builder example

In this section, we are going to apply the builder pattern to our car software. We have a `Car` class and we need to create instances of it. Depending on the components we add to the car, we can build sedan cars and sports cars. When we start designing our software, we realize the following:

- The `Car` class is quite complex, and creating class objects is a complex operation too. Adding all of the instantiation logic in the `Car` constructor will make the class quite big.

- We need to build several types of cars. Usually, for this scenario, we add several different constructors, but our intuition is telling us that this is not the best solution.
- In the future, we probably need to build different types of car objects. The demand for semi-automatic cars is quite high already, so in the near future we should be ready to extend our code without modifying it.

We are going to create the following class structure:

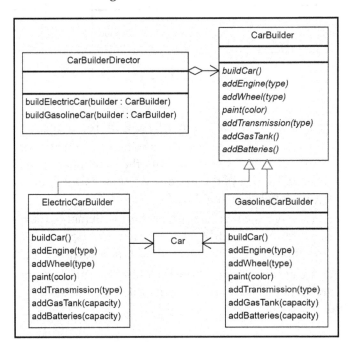

CarBuilder is the builder base class and it contains four abstract methods. We created two concrete builders: ElectricCarBuilder and GasolineCarBuilder. Each of the concrete builders has to implement all of the abstract methods. The methods that are not required, such as addGasTank for the ElectricCarBuilder, are left empty or they can throw an exception. Electric and gasoline cars have different internal structures.

The Director class uses the builders to create new car objects. buildElectricCar and buildGasolineCar may be similar, with slight differences:

```
public Car buildElectricCar(CarBuilder builder)
{
  builder.buildCar();
  builder.addEngine("Electric 150 kW");
```

```
    builder.addBatteries("1500 kWh");
    builder.addTransmission("Manual");
    for (int i = 0; i < 4; i++)
    builder.addWheel("20x12x30");
    builder.paint("red");
    return builder.getCar();
}
```

But let's assume we want to build a hybrid car with an electric and a gasoline engine:

```
public Car buildHybridCar(CarBuilder builder)
{
    builder.buildCar();
    builder.addEngine("Electric 150 kW");
    builder.addBatteries("1500 kWh");
    builder.addTransmission("Manual");
    for (int i = 0; i < 4; i++)
    builder.addWheel("20x12x30");
    builder.paint("red");
    builder.addGasTank("1500 kWh");
    builder.addEngine("Gas 1600cc");
    return builder.getCar();
}
```

Simplified builder pattern

In some implementations of the builder pattern, the Director class can be removed. In our class example, the logic it encapsulates is quite simple, so in that case we don't really need a director. In this case, the simplified builder pattern would look like this:

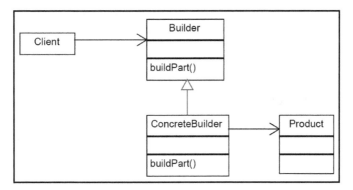

The code that was implemented in the `Director` class is simply moved to the `Client`. This change is not recommended when the `Builder` and `Product` classes are too complex or when the builder is used to build an object from a stream of data.

Anonymous builders with method chaining

As described previously, the most intuitive way to deal with objects from the same class that should take different forms is to create several constructors to instantiate them for each scenario. Using builder patterns to avoid this is a good practice. In *Effective Java,* Joshua Bloch proposes using inner builder classes and method chaining to replace multiple constructors.

Method chaining is a technique to return the current object (`this`) from certain methods. This way, the methods can be invoked in a chain. For example:

```
public Builder setColor()
{
  // set color
  return this;
}
```

After we have defined more methods like this, we can invoke them in a chain:

```
builder.setColor("Blue")
.setEngine("1500cc")
.addTank("50")
.addTransmission("auto")
.build();
```

But, in our case, we are going to make `builder` an inner class of the `Car` object. So, when we need a new client, we can do the following:

```
Car car = new Car.Builder.setColor("Blue")
.setEngine("1500cc")
.addTank("50")
.addTransmission("auto")
.build();
```

Prototype pattern

The prototype pattern is a pattern that seems more complicated than it really is. Practically, it is just a method to clone objects. Why would we need to clone objects when, these days, instantiating objects is not too costly in terms of performance? There are several situations in which it is required to clone objects that are already instantiated:

- When the creation of a new object relies on an external resource or a hardware-intensive operation
- When we need a copy of the same object with the same state without having to redo all of the operations to get to that state
- When we need an instance of an object without knowing to which concrete class it belongs

Let's look at the following class diagram:

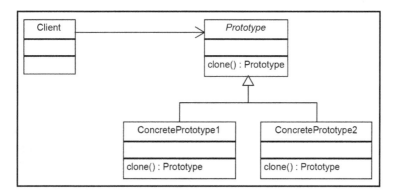

In the prototype pattern, the following classes are involved:

- `Prototype`: This is the base class, or an interface that declares the `clone()` method that derived objects have to implement. In a simple scenario, we may not have a base class, and a direct concrete class is sufficient.
- `ConcretePrototype`: These classes implement or extend the `clone()` method. This method should always be implemented because it returns a new instance of its type. If the `clone()` method was implemented in the base class and we didn't implement it in `ConcretePrototype`, when we invoked the `clone()` method on a `ConcretePrototype` object, it would return a base `Prototype` object.

The `clone()` method can be declared in an interface so classes implementing the method have to implement the method. This enforcement is done at compile time. However, it is not enforced on classes inherited from classes that implement the `clone()` method in hierarchies with more than one level.

Shallow clone versus deep clone

When cloning objects, we should be aware of the deepness of cloning. When we clone an object that contains simple datatypes, such as `int` and `float`, or immutable objects, such as strings, we should simply copy those fields to the new object, and that's it.

A problem arises when our objects contain references to other objects. For example, if we have to implement a clone method for a `Car` class that has an engine and a list of four wheels, we should create not only a new `Car` object but also a new `Engine` and four new `Wheel` objects. After all, two cars cannot share the same engine and the same wheels. This is called a **deep clone**.

Shallow cloning is a method of cloning only the object that is the subject of cloning. For example, if we have to implement a clone method for a `Student` object, we are not going to clone the `Course` object it points to. More than one `Student` object can point to the same `Course` object.

In practice, we should decide whether we need deep, shallow, or mixed cloning based on each scenario. Usually, shallow cloning corresponds to the aggregation relation described in `Chapter 1`, *From Object-Oriented to Functional Programming*, and deep cloning to the composition relation.

Object pool pattern

The instantiation of objects is one of the most costly operations in terms of performance. While in the past this could have been an issue, nowadays we shouldn't be concerned about it. However, when we deal with objects that encapsulate external resources, such as database connections, the creation of new objects becomes expensive.

The solution is to implement a mechanism that reuses and shares objects that are expensive to create. This solution is called the object pool pattern and it has the following structure:

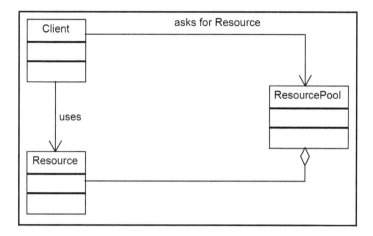

The classes that are used in the object pool pattern are the following:

- ResourcePool: A class that encapsulates the logic to hold and manage a list of resources.
- Resource: A class that encapsulates a limited resource. The Resource classes are always referenced by the ResourcePool, so they will never be garbage collected as long as the ResourcePool is not de-allocated.
- Client: The class that uses resources.

When a Client needs a new Resource, it asks for it from the ResourcePool. The pool checks and takes the first available resource and returns it to the client:

```
public Resource acquireResource()
{
  if ( available.size() <= 0 )
  {
    Resource resource = new Resource();
    inuse.add(resource);
    return resource;
  }
  else
  {
    return available.remove(0);
  }
}
```

Then, when the `Client` finishes using the `Resource`, it releases it. The resource is added back to the tool so that it can be reused.

```
public void releaseResource(Resource resource)
{
   available.add(resource);
}
```

One of the best examples of resource pooling is database connection pooling. We maintain a pool of database connections and let the code use connections from this pool.

Summary

In this chapter, we covered creational design patterns. We talked about variations of the singleton, factory, builder, prototype, and object pool patterns. All these patterns are used to instantiate new objects and give code flexibility and reusability while creating objects. In the next chapter, we will cover behavioral patterns. While creational patterns help us to manage the creation of objects, behavioral patterns provide an easy way to manage the behavior of objects.

3
Behavioral Patterns

The objective of this chapter is to learn about behavioral patterns. Behavioral patterns are patterns that focus on object interaction, communication, and control flows. Most behavioral patterns are based on composition and delegation rather than inheritance. We will look at the following behavioral patterns in this chapter:

- The chain-of-responsibility pattern
- The command pattern
- The interpreter pattern
- The iterator pattern
- The observer pattern
- The mediator pattern
- The memento pattern
- The state pattern
- The strategy pattern
- The template method pattern
- The null object pattern
- The visitor pattern

The chain-of-responsibility pattern

Computer software is for processing information, and there are different ways of structuring and processing that information. We already know that when we talk about object-oriented programming, we should assign a single responsibility to each class in order to make our design easy to extend and maintain.

Consider a scenario where multiple types of operations can be performed on a set of data that comes with a client request. Instead of adding information about all the operations in a single class, we can maintain different classes responsible for the different types of operations. This helps us keep our code loosely coupled and clean.

These classes are called handlers. The first handler will receive the request and take a call if it needs to perform an action, or pass it on to the second handler. Similarly, the second handler checks and can pass on the request to the next handler in the chain.

Intent

The chain-of-responsibility pattern chains the handlers in such a way that they will be able to process the request or pass it on if they are not able to do it.

Implementation

The following class diagram describes the structure and the actors of the chain-of-responsibility pattern:

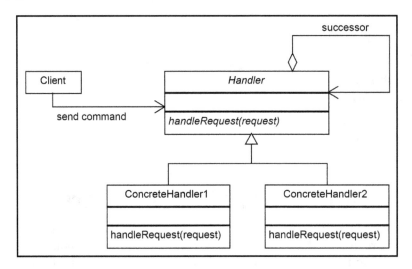

The following classes are involved in the preceding diagram:

- **Client**: This is the main structure of the application that uses the pattern. It's responsible for instantiating a chain of handlers and then for invoking the `handleRequest` method on the first object.
- **Handler**: This is the abstract class from which all the concrete handlers have to be inherited. It has a `handleRequest` method, which receives the request that should be processed.
- **ConcreteHandlers**: These are the concrete classes which implement a `handleRequest` method for each case. Each `ConcreteHandler` keeps a reference to the next `ConcreteHandler` in the chain and has to check whether it can process the request; otherwise, it has to pass it on to the next `ConcreteHandler` in the chain.

Each handler should implement a method that is used by the client to set the next handler to which it should pass the request if it's not able to process it. This method can be added to the base `Handler` class:

```
protected Handler successor;
public void setSuccessor(Handler successor)
{
   this.successor = successor;
}
```

In each `ConcreteHandler` class, we have the following code, which checks whether it can handle the request; otherwise, it passes it on:

```
public void handleRequest(Request request)
{
   if (canHandle(request))
   {
     //code to handle the request
   }
   else
   {
     successor.handleRequest();
   }
}
```

The client is responsible for building the chain of handlers before invoking the head of the chain. The call will be propagated until it finds the right handler that can process the request.

Let's take our car service application example. We realize that each time a broken car comes in, it is first checked by the mechanic, who fixes it if the problem is in their area of expertise. If they're not able to, they send it on to the electrician. If they're not able to fix it, they pass it on to the next expert. Here's how the diagram would look:

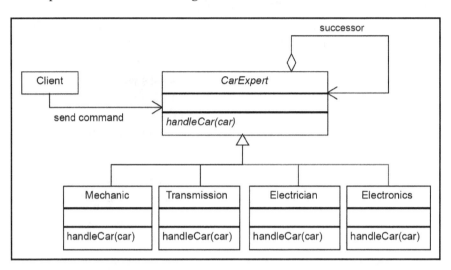

Applicability and examples

What follows is the applicability and examples of the chain-of-responsibility pattern:

- **Event handlers**: For example, most GUI frameworks use the chain-of-responsibility pattern to handle events. Let's say, for example, a window contains a panel that contains some buttons. We have to write the event handler of the button. If we decide to skip it and pass it on, the next one in the chain will be able to handle the request: the panel. If the panel skips it, it will go to the window.

- **Log handlers**: Similar to the event handlers, each log handler will log a specific request based on its status, or it will pass it on to the next handler.

- **Servlets**: In Java, `javax.servlet.Filter` (`http://docs.oracle.com/javaee/7/api/javax/servlet/Filter.html`) is used to filter requests or responses. The `doFilter` method also receives the filter chain as a parameter, and it can pass the request on.

The command pattern

One of the most important things to do in object-oriented programming is to adopt a design that lets us decouple the code. For example, let's imagine that we need to develop a complex application in which we can draw graphic shapes: points, lines, segments, circles, rectangles, and many more.

Along with the code to draw all kinds of shapes, we need to implement many operations to handle the menu operations. In order to make our application maintainable, we are going to create a unified way to define all those *commands* in such a way that it will hide the implementation details from the rest of the application (which plays the client role).

Intent

The command pattern does the following:

- Provides a unified way to encapsulate a command along with the required parameters to execute an action
- Allows the handling of commands, such as storing them in queues

Implementation

The class diagram of the command pattern is as follows:

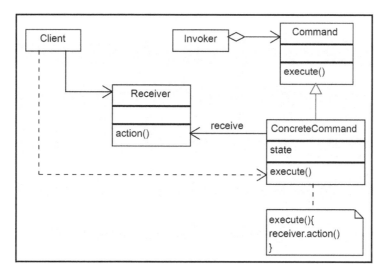

We can distinguish the following actors in the preceding implementation diagram:

- **Command**: This is the abstraction that represents the encapsulation of a command. It declares the abstract method executed, which should be implemented by all the concrete commands.
- **ConcreteCommand**: This is the actual implementation of the **Command**. It has to execute the command and deal with the parameters associated with each concrete command. It delegates the command to the receiver.
- **Receiver**: This is the class responsible for executing the action associated with the command.
- **Invoker**: This is the class that triggers the command. This is usually an external event, such as a user action.
- **Client**: This is the actual class that instantiates the concrete command objects and their receivers.

Initially, our impulse is to deal with all possible commands in a big `if-else` block:

```
public void performAction(ActionEvent e)
{
  Object obj = e.getSource();
  if (obj = fileNewMenuItem)
  doFileNewAction();
  else if (obj = fileOpenMenuItem)
  doFileOpenAction();
  else if (obj = fileOpenRecentMenuItem)
  doFileOpenRecentAction();
  else if (obj = fileSaveMenuItem)
  doFileSaveAction();
}
```

However, we may decide to apply the command pattern for the drawing application. We start by creating a command interface:

```
public interface Command
{
  public void execute();
}
```

The next step is to define all the objects, such as menu items and buttons, as classes, implementing the command interface and the `execute()` method:

```
public class OpenMenuItem extends JMenuItem implements Command
{
  public void execute()
  {
    // code to open a document
  }
}
```

After we have repeated the previous operation, creating a class for each possible action, we replace the `if-else` block from the naive implementation with the following one:

```
public void performAction(ActionEvent e)
{
  Command command = (Command)e.getSource();
  command.execute();
}
```

We can see from our code that the invoker (the client that triggers the `performAction` method) and the receivers (the classes implementing the command interface) are decoupled. We can easily extend our code without changing it.

Applicability and examples

The applicability and examples of the command pattern are as follows:

- **Undo/redo operations**: The command pattern allows us to store the command object in a queue. This way, we can implement undo and redo operations.
- **Composite commands**: Complex commands can be composed of simple commands using the composite pattern, and are run in a sequential order. In this way, we can build macros in an object-oriented-design manner.
- **The asynchronous method invocation**: The command pattern is used in multithreading applications. Command objects can be executed in the background in separate threads. The java.lang.Runnable is a command interface.

In the following code, the runnable interface acts as a command interface, and is implemented by RunnableThread:

```
class RunnableThread implements Runnable
{
  public void run()
  {
    // the command implementation code
  }
}
```

The client invokes the command to start a new thread:

```
public class ClientThread
{
  public static void main(String a[])
  {
    RunnableThread mrt = new RunnableThread();
    Thread t = new Thread(mrt);
    t.start();
  }
}
```

The interpreter pattern

Computers are supposed to interpret sentences or evaluate expressions. If we have to write a sequence of code that is supposed to deal with such a requirement, first of all, we need to know the structure; we need to have an internal representation of the expression or the sentence. In many situations, the most appropriate structure to use is a composite one based on the composite pattern. We will further discuss the composite pattern in Chapter 4, *Structural Patterns*, for now, we can think of composite representation as grouping objects of a similar nature together.

Intent

The interpreter pattern defines the representation of the grammar along with the interpretation.

Implementation

The interpreter pattern uses the composite pattern to define the internal representation of the object structure. In addition to that, it adds the implementation to interpret an expression and to convert it to the internal structure. For this reason, the interpreter pattern falls within the behavioral patterns category. The class diagram is as follows:

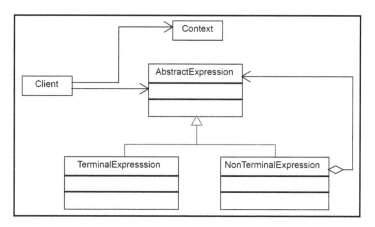

The interpreter pattern is composed of the following classes:

- **Context**: This is used to encapsulate the information that is global to the interpreter and needs to be accessed by all concrete interpreters.
- **AbstractExpression**: An abstract class or interface that declares the interpret method executed, which should be implemented by all the concrete interpreters.
- **TerminalExpression**: An interpreter class which implements the operations associated with the terminal symbols of the grammar. This class must always be implemented and instantiated, as it signals the end of the expression.
- **NonTerminalExpression**: These are classes that implement different rules or symbols of the grammar. For each one, there should be one class created.

The interpreter pattern is used in practice to interpret regular expressions. It's a good exercise to implement the interpreter pattern for such a scenario; however, we'll choose a simple grammar for our example. We are going to apply it to parse a simple function with one variable: f(x).

To make it even simpler, we are going to choose the Reverse Polish notation. This is a notation in which the operands are added at the end of the operators. The *1 + 2* becomes *1 2 +*; *(1+2)*3* becomes *1 2 + 3 **. The advantage is that we no longer need parentheses, so it simplifies our task.

The following code creates an interface for expressions:

```
public interface Expression
{
  public float interpret();
}
```

Now we need to implement the concrete classes. We need the following elements:

- **Number**: This will interpret the numbers
- **Operator classes (+,-,*,/)**: For the following example, we will use plus (+) and minus (-):

```
public class Number implements Expression
{
  private float number;
  public Number(float number)
  {
    this.number = number;
  }
  public float interpret()
  {
    return number;
  }
}
```

Now we reach the difficult part. We need to implement the operators. The operators are composite expressions, which are composed of two expressions:

```
public class Plus implements Expression
{
  Expression left;
  Expression right;
  public Plus(Expression left, Expression right)
  {
    this.left = left;
    this.right = right;
  }
  public float interpret()
  {
    return left.interpret() + right.interpret();
  }
}
```

Similarly, we have a minus implementation as follows:

```java
public class Minus implements Expression
{
  Expression left;
  Expression right;
  public Minus(Expression left, Expression right)
  {
    this.left = left;
    this.right = right;
  }
  public float interpret()
  {
    return right.interpret() - left.interpret();
  }
}
```

We can see now that we've created the classes that allow us to build a tree in which operations are nodes, and variables and numbers are leaves. The structure can be quite complex and can be used to interpret an expression.

Now we have to write the code to build the tree using the classes we've created:

```java
public class Evaluator
{
  public float evaluate(String expression)
  {
    Stack<Expression> stack = new Stack<Expression>();
    float result =0;
    for (String token : expression.split(" "))
    {
      if  (isOperator(token))
      {
        Expression exp = null;
        if(token.equals("+"))
        exp = stack.push(new Plus(stack.pop(), stack.pop()));
        else if (token.equals("-"))
        exp = stack.push(new Minus(stack.pop(), stack.pop()));
        if(null!=exp)
        {
          result = exp.interpret();
          stack.push(new Number(result));
        }
      }
      if  (isNumber(token))
      {
        stack.push(new Number(Float.parseFloat(token)));
```

```
        }
    }
    return result;
}
private boolean isNumber(String token)
{
    try
    {
        Float.parseFloat(token);
        return true;
    }
    catch(NumberFormatException nan)
    {
        return false;
    }
}
private boolean isOperator(String token)
{
    if(token.equals("+") || token.equals("-"))
    return true;
    return false;
}
public static void main(String s[])
{
    Evaluator eval = new Evaluator();
    System.out.println(eval.evaluate("2 3 +"));
    System.out.println(eval.evaluate("4 3 -"));
    System.out.println(eval.evaluate("4 3 - 2 +"));
}
}
```

Applicability and examples

The interpreter pattern can be used whenever an expression should be interpreted and transformed to its internal representation. The pattern cannot be applied to complex grammars since the internal representation is based on a composite pattern.

Java implements the interpreter pattern in `java.util.Parser` and it is used to interpret regular expressions. First, when a regular expression is interpreted, a matcher object is returned. The matcher uses the internal structure that was created by the pattern class based on the regular expression:

```
Pattern p = Pattern. compile("a*b");
Matcher m = p.matcher ("aaaaab");
boolean b = m.matches();
```

The iterator pattern

The iterator pattern is probably one of the most well-known patterns in Java. Some Java programmers are using it without being aware that the collection package is an implementation of the iterator pattern, regardless of the type of the collection: array, list, set, or any other types.

The fact that we can deal in the same way with a collection, regardless of whether it's a list or an array, is because it provides a mechanism to iterate through its elements without exposing its internal structure. What's more, the same unified mechanism is used by different types of collections. The mechanism is called the iterator pattern.

Intent

The iterator pattern provides a way to traverse the elements of an aggregate object sequentially without exposing its internal representation.

Implementation

The iterator pattern is based on two abstract classes or interfaces, which can be implemented by pairs of concrete classes. The class diagram is as follows:

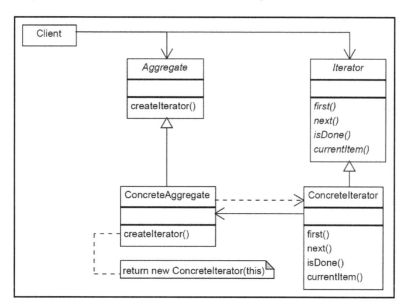

The following classes are used in the iterator pattern:

- **Aggregate**: The abstract class that should be implemented by all the classes and can be traversed by an iterator. This corresponds to the `java.util.Collection` interface.
- **Iterator**: This is the iterator abstraction that defines the operations to traverse the aggregate object along with the one to return the object.
- **ConcreteAggregate**: Concrete aggregates can implement internally different structures, but expose the concrete iterator, which deals with traversing the aggregates.
- **ConcreteIterator**: This is the concrete iterator that deals with a specific concrete aggregate class. In practice, for each **ConcreteAggregate,** we have to implement a **ConcreteIterator**.

Using the iterators in Java is probably one of the things every programmer does in daily life. Let's see how we can implement an iterator. First of all, we should define a simple iterator interface:

```
public interface Iterator
{
  public Object next();
  public boolean hasNext();
}
We create the aggregate:
public interface Aggregate
{
public Iterator createIterator();
}
```

Then we implement a simple `Aggregator`, which maintains an array of String values:

```
public class StringArray implements Aggregate
{
  private String values[];
  public StringArray(String[] values)
  {
    this.values = values;
  }
  public Iterator createIterator()
  {
    return (Iterator) new StringArrayIterator();
  }
  private class StringArrayIterator implements Iterator
  {
    private int position;
```

```java
    public boolean hasNext()
    {
      return (position < values.length);
    }
    public String next()
    {
      if (this.hasNext())
      return values[position++];
      else
      return null;
    }
  }
}
```

We nested the iterator class in the aggregate. This is the best option because the iterator needs access to the internal variables of the aggregator. We can see here how it looks:

```java
String arr[]= {"a", "b", "c", "d"};
StringArray strarr = new StringArray(arr);
for (Iterator it = strarr.createIterator(); it.hasNext();)
System.out.println(it.next());
```

Applicability and examples

Iterators are popular in most programming languages these days. It is probably most widely used in Java, along with the collections package. It is also implemented at the language level when a collection is traversed with the following loop construction:

```java
for (String item : strCollection)
System.out.println(item);
```

The iterator pattern can be implemented using the generics mechanism. This way, we can make sure we can avoid runtime errors generated by forced castings.

Good practice when implementing new containers and iterators in Java is to implement the existing `java.util.Iterator<E>` and `java.util.Collection<E>` classes. When we need aggregators with specific behaviors, we should also consider extending one of the classes that were implemented in the `java.collection` package instead of creating a new one.

The observer pattern

As we advance in this book, we keep mentioning how important decoupling is. When we reduce dependencies, we can extend, develop, and test different modules without having to know the implementation details of other modules. All we have to know is the abstraction they implement.

However, modules should work together in practice. And it's not uncommon that changes in one object are known by another object. For example, if we implement a `car` class in a game, the engine of the car should know when the accelerator changes its position. The naive solution would be to have an `engine` class that checks from time to time the accelerator position to see whether it has changed. A smarter approach would be to make the accelerator call the engine to inform it about the changes. But this is not enough if we want to have well-designed code.

If the `Accelerator` class keeps a reference to the `Engine` class, what happens when we need to display on screen the position of `Accelerator`? This is the best solution: instead of making the accelerator dependent on the engine, we should make both of them rely on abstractions.

Intent

The observer pattern makes the state changes of one object observable to other objects that are registered to be informed.

Implementation

The class diagram of the observer pattern is as follows:

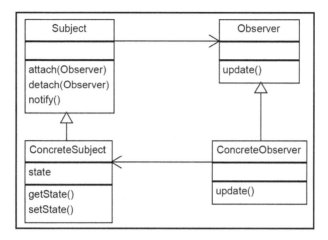

The observer pattern relies on the following classes:

- **Subject**: This is usually an interface that must be implemented by the classes and should be observable. The observers that should be notified are registered using the **attach** method. When they no longer have to be informed about the changes, they are deregistered using the **detach** method.
- **ConcreteSubject**: This is a class that implements the subject interface. It handles the list of observers and it updates them about the changes.
- **Observer**: This is an interface that is implemented by the objects that should be updated by the changes in the subject. Each observer should implement the **update** method, which informs them about the new state changes.

The mediator pattern

In many cases, when we design and develop software applications, we encounter many scenarios where we have modules and objects that have to communicate with one another. The easiest approach would be to make them in such a way that they know each other and can send messages directly.

However, this might create a mess. If we imagine, for example, a communication app in which each client has to connect to another one, it doesn't make sense for a client to manage many connections. A better solution would be to connect to a central server and for the server to manage the communication between the clients. The client sends the message to the server and the server keeps the connection active to all the clients, and it can broadcast messages to all required recipients.

Another example is where a specialized class is required to mediate between different controls, such as buttons, dropdowns, and list controls, in a graphical interface. For example, the graphical controls in a GUI can hold a reference to each other in order to invoke their methods reciprocally. But obviously, this will create an extremely coupled code in which each control depends on all the others. A better approach would be to make the parent responsible for broadcasting messages to all the required controls when something needs to be done. When something modifies in a control, it will notify the window, which will check which controls need to be informed and then inform them.

Intent

The mediator pattern defines an object that encapsulates how a set of objects interacts, reducing their dependency on one another.

Implementation

The mediator pattern is based on two abstractions: **Mediator** and **Colleague**, as shown in the following class diagram:

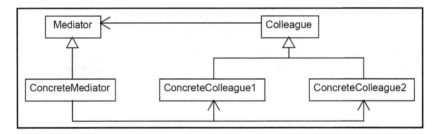

The mediator pattern relies on the following classes:

- **Mediator**: This defines how the participants are interacting. The operations declared in this interface or abstract class are specific to each scenario.
- **ConcreteMediator**: This implements the operations declared by the mediator.
- **Colleague**: This is an abstract class or interface that defines how the participants that need mediating should interact.
- **ConcreteColleague**: These are the concrete classes implementing the **Colleague** interface.

Applicability and examples

The mediator pattern should be used when there are lots of entities interacting in a similar manner and those entities should be decoupled.

The mediator pattern is used in Java libraries to implement `java.util.Timer`. The `timer` class can be used to schedule threads to run one time or repeatedly at regular intervals. The thread objects correspond to the `ConcreteColleague` class. The `timer` class implements methods to manage the execution of background tasks.

The memento pattern

Encapsulation is one of the fundamental principles of object-oriented design. We also know that each class should have a single responsibility. As we add functionality to our object, we might realize that we need to save its internal state to be able to restore it at a later stage. If we implement such functionality directly in the class, the class might become too complex and we might end up breaking the single responsibility principle. At the same time, encapsulation prevents us having direct access to the internal state of the object we need to memorize.

Intent

The memento pattern is used to save the internal state of an object without breaking its encapsulation, and to restore its state at a later stage.

Implementation

The memento pattern relies on three classes: **Originator**, **Memento**, and **Caretaker**, as shown in the following class diagram:

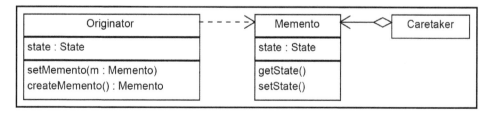

The memento pattern relies on the following classes:

- **Originator**: The originator is the object for which we need to memorize the state in case we need to restore it at some point.
- **Caretaker**: This is the class responsible for triggering the changes in the originator or for triggering an action through which the originator returns to a previous state.
- **Memento**: This is the class responsible for storing the internal state of the originator. Memento provides two methods by which to set and get a state, but those methods should be hidden from the caretaker.

In practice, memento is much easier than it sounds. Let's apply it to our car service application. Our mechanic has to test each car. They use an automatic device that measures all the outputs of the car for different parameters (speed, gears, brakes, and so on). They perform all the tests and have to re-check those that look suspicious.

We start by creating the `originator` class. We'll name it `CarOriginator` and we'll add two member variables. `state` represents the parameters of the car when the test is run. This is the state of the object we want to save; the second member variable is result. This is the measured output of the car and we don't need to store this in the memento. Here is the originator with an empty-nested memento:

```
public class CarOriginator
{
  private String state;
  public void setState(String state)
  {
    this.state = state;
  }
  public String getState()
  {
    return this.state;
  }
  public Memento saveState()
  {
    return new Memento(this.state);
  }
  public void restoreState(Memento memento)
  {
    this.state = memento.getState();
  }
  /**
  * Memento class
  */
  public static class Memento
```

```
  {
    private final String state;
    public Memento(String state)
    {
      this.state = state;
    }
    private String getState()
    {
      return state;
    }
  }
}
```

Now we run the car tests for different states:

```
public class CarCaretaker
{
  public static void main(String s[])
  {
    new CarCaretaker().runMechanicTest();
  }
  public void runMechanicTest()
  {
    CarOriginator.Memento savedState = new CarOriginator.
    Memento("");
    CarOriginator originator = new CarOriginator();
    originator.setState("State1");
    originator.setState("State2");
    savedState = originator.saveState();
    originator.setState("State3");
    originator.restoreState(savedState);
    System.out.println("final state:" + originator.getState());
  }
}
```

Applicability

The memento pattern is used whenever rollback operations need to be implemented. It can be used in all kinds of atomic transactions in which the object must be reverted to the initial state if one of the actions fails.

The state pattern

A finite state machine is an important concept in computer science. It has a strong mathematical base and it represents an abstract machine that can be in a finite number of states. Finite state machines are used in all fields of computer science.

The state pattern is just an implementation of a finite state machine in object-oriented design. The class diagram is as follows:

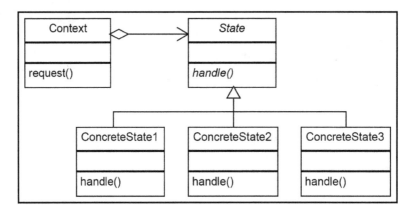

The strategy pattern

A particular situation specific to behavioral patterns is when we need to change the way to solve a problem with another one. As we already learned in the first chapter, changing is bad, while extending is good. So, instead of replacing a portion of code with another one, we can encapsulate it in a class. Then we can create an abstraction of that class on which our code depends. From that point, our code becomes very flexible, as we can now use any class that implements the abstraction we just created.

Intent

The strategy pattern defines a family of algorithms, encapsulating each one, and makes them interchangeable.

Implementation

The structure of the strategy pattern is practically the same as the state pattern. However, the implementation and the intent are totally different:

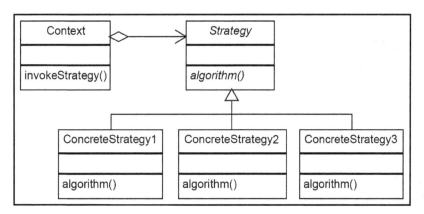

The strategy pattern is quite simple:

- **Strategy**: The abstraction of a specific strategy
- **ConcreteStrategy**: The classes that implement the abstract strategy
- **Context**: The class that runs a specific strategy

The template method pattern

The template method pattern, as the name suggests, provides a template for code, which can be filled in by developers implementing different functionalities. The easiest way to understand this is to think in terms of HTML templates. Most of the websites you visit follow some kind of template. For example, there is usually a header, a footer, and a sidebar, and in between, we have the core content. That means the template is defined with a header, footer, and sidebars, and every content writer can use this template to add their content.

Intent

The idea of using the template method pattern is to avoid writing duplicate code so that developers can focus on core logic.

Implementation

The template method pattern is best implemented using an abstract class. The areas for which we know about the implementation will be provided; the default implementation and the areas that are to be kept open for implementation are marked abstract.

For example, think of a database fetch query at a very high level. We need to execute the following steps:

1. Create a connection
2. Create a query
3. Execute the query
4. Parse and return the data
5. Close the connection

We can see that creating and closing the connection part will always remain the same. So, we can add this as part of the template implementation. The remaining methods can be implemented independently for different needs.

The null object pattern

The null object pattern is one of the lightest patterns covered in this book. Sometimes, it is considered just a particular case of the strategy pattern, but it has its own section, given the importance it has in practice.

If we develop programs using a test-driven approach, or if we simply want to develop a module without having the rest of the application, we can simply replace the classes we don't have with a mock class, which has the same structure but does nothing.

Implementation

In the following diagram, we can see that we simply create a **NullClass**, which can replace the real class in our program. As mentioned before, this is just a particular case of the strategy pattern in which we choose the strategy of doing nothing. The class diagram is as follows:

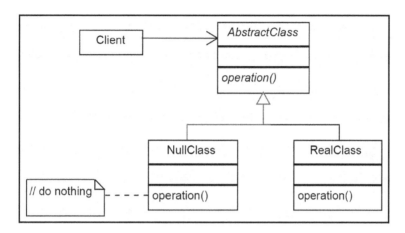

The visitor pattern

Let's go back to the shapes application we introduced when talking about the command pattern. We applied the command pattern, so we have to redo the operations implemented. It's time to add a save functionality.

We might think that if we add an abstract Save method to the base shape class and if we extend it for each of the shapes, we have the problem solved. This solution is maybe the most intuitive, but not the best. First of all, each class should have a single responsibility.

Secondly, what happens if we need to change the format in which we want to save each shape? If we are implementing the same methods to generate an XML out, do we then have to change to JSON format? This design definitely does not follow the open/closed principle.

Intent

The visitor pattern separates an operation from the object structure on which it operates, allowing the addition of new operations without changing the structure classes.

Implementation

The visitor pattern defines a set of operations in a single class: it defines one method for each type of object from the structure it has to operate on. Adding a new set of operations can be done simply by creating another visitor. The class diagram is as follows:

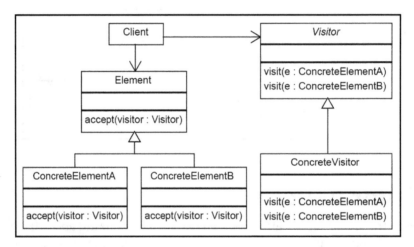

The visitor pattern is based on the following classes:

- **Element**: This represents the base class for the object structure. All the classes in the structure are derived from it and they must implement the **accept(visitor: Visitor)** method.
- **ConcreteElementA and ConcreteElementB**: These are concrete classes to which we want to add external operations implemented in the **Visitor** class.
- **Visitor**: This is the base **Visitor** class, which declares a method corresponding to each **ConcreteElementA**. The name of the method is the same, but each method is differentiated by the type it accepts. We can adopt this solution because in Java, we can have methods with the same name and different signatures; but, if needed, we can declare methods with different names.
- **ConcreteVisitor**: This is the implementation of the visitor. When we need a separate set of operations, we simply create another visitor.

Summary

In this section, we discussed various behavioral patterns. We looked at some of the most commonly used behavioral patterns, such as the chain-of-responsibility, the command pattern, the interpreter pattern, and so on. These patterns help us manage the behavior of objects in a controlled manner. In the next chapter, we will look into structural patterns, which help us manage complex structures.

4
Structural Patterns

The objective of this chapter is to learn about structural patterns. Structural patterns are patterns that focus on creating complex structures by making use of relations between objects and classes. Most structural patterns are based on inheritance. In this chapter, we will focus only on the following GOF patterns:

- The adapter pattern
- The proxy pattern
- The bridge pattern
- The decorator pattern
- The composite pattern
- The façade pattern
- The flyweight pattern

There are other identified structural patterns that we may not be able to cover in detail, but it is worth knowing about them. These are the following:

- **Marker interface**: This uses an empty interface to mark specific classes (such as serializable), thus making searching by interface name possible. For more information, please read the article, *Item 37 - using marker interfaces to define types*, at `http://thefinestartist.com/effective-java/37`, which makes reference to *Effective Java (2nd Edition)*, written by Joshua Bloch.
- **Module**: This groups classes together to implement the concept of software modules. A modular architecture contains multiple patterns, which are explained in a clear way by Kirk Knoernschild at `https://dzone.com/refcardz/patterns-modular-architecture`. Java 9 module is an example of this pattern—read more at `https://labs.consol.de/development/2017/02/13/getting-started-with-java9-modules.html`.
- **Extension object**: This changes at runtime the existing object interface. More information is available at `http://www.brockmann-consult.de/beam-wiki/display/BEAM/Extension+Object+Pattern`.

- **Twin**: This adds multiple inheritance capabilities to languages that do not support it. Java 8 has support for multiple inheritances of type by the addition of default methods. Even so, the twin pattern can still be useful in some cases. The Java design pattern com site has a good description of the twin pattern at `http:/ /java-design-patterns.com/patterns/twin/`.

Adapter pattern

The adapter pattern provides a solution for code reusability; it adapts/wraps existing old code to new interfaces, interfaces that were unknown at the design time of the original code. In 1987, when the PS/2 port was designed, no one imagined that it would be connected to a USB bus designed nine years later. Yet we can still use an old PS/2 keyboard in our newest computer by connecting it to the USB port.

The adapter pattern is commonly used when working with legacy code, since by wrapping the existing code and adapting it to the new code interface, we instantly gain access to the old, already-tested, functionality. This can be done either by using multiple inheritances, made possible in Java 8 by default interface implementation, or by using composition, where the old object becomes a class attribute. The adapter pattern is also known as a **wrapper**.

In cases where the old code needs to make use of the new code, and vice-versa, we need to use a special adapter called a two-way adapter, which implements both interfaces (the old and the new one).

The `java.io.InputStreamReader` and `java.io.OutputStreamWriter` classes from JDK are adapters, since they adapt input/output stream objects from JDK1.0 to reader/writer objects defined later, in JDK1.1.

Intent

The intent is to adopt an existing old interface to a new client interface. The goal is to reuse as much as possible the old and already tested code, while being free to make changes to the new interface.

Implementation

The following UML diagram models the interaction between the new client code and the adapted one. The adapter pattern is usually implemented in other languages by using multiple inheritance, which is partially possible starting from Java 8. We will use another approach, which works with older Java versions too; we'll use aggregation. It is more restrictive than inheritance since we are not going to get access to protected content, just the adapter public interface:

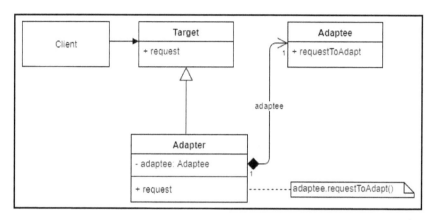

We can distinguish between the following actors from the implementation diagram:

- Client: The code client
- Adapter: The adapter class that forwards the calls to the adaptee
- Adaptee: The old code that needs to be adapted
- Target: The new interface to support

Examples

The following code simulates the use of a PS/2 keyboard in a USB bus. It defines a PS/2 keyboard (adaptee), a USB device interface (target), a PS2ToUSBAdapter (adapter), and the wires to link in order to make the device work:

```
package gof.structural.adapter;
import java.util.Arrays;
import java.util.Collections;
import java.util.List;
class WireCap
{
```

```
      WireCap link = WireCap.LooseCap;
      private Wire wire;
      publicstatic WireCap LooseCap = new WireCap(null);
      public WireCap(Wire wire)
      {
        this.wire = wire;
      }
      publicvoid addLinkTo(WireCap link)
      {
        this.link = link;
      }
      public Wire getWire()
      {
        return wire;
      }
      public String toString()
      {
        if (link.equals(WireCap.LooseCap))
        return "WireCap belonging to LooseCap";
        return "WireCap belonging to " + wire + " is linked to " +
        link.getWire();
      }
      public WireCap getLink()
      {
        return link;
      }
    }
```

The `WireCap` class models, as the name suggests, the ends of each wire. By default, all wires are loose; therefore, we need a way to signal this. This is done by using the Null object pattern—the `LooseCap` is our null object (a null replacement, which does not throw `NullPointerException`). Take a look at this code:

```
  class Wire
  {
    private String name;
    private WireCap left;
    private WireCap right;
    public Wire(String name)
    {
      this.name = name;
      this.left = new WireCap(this);
      this.right = new WireCap(this);
    }
    publicvoid linkLeftTo(Wire link)
    {
      left.addLinkTo(link.getRightWireCap());
```

```
      link.getRightWireCap().addLinkTo(left);
   }
   public WireCap getRightWireCap()
   {
      return right;
   }
   publicvoid printWireConnectionsToRight()
   {
      Wire wire = this;
      while (wire.hasLinkedRightCap())
      {
         wire.printRightCap();
         wire = wire.getRightLink();
      }
   }
   public Wire getRightLink()
   {
      return getRightWireCap().getLink().getWire();
   }
   publicvoid printRightCap()
   {
      System.out.println(getRightWireCap());
   }
   publicboolean hasLinkedRightCap()
   {
      return !getRightWireCap().link.equals(WireCap.LooseCap);
   }
   public String getName()
   {
      return name;
   }
   public String toString()
   {
      return "Wire " + name;
   }
}
```

The `Wire` class models the wires from a USB or PS/2 device. It has two ends, which by default are loose, as shown in the following code:

```
class USBPort
{
   publicfinal Wire wireRed = new Wire("USB Red5V");
   publicfinal Wire wireWhite = new Wire("USB White");
   publicfinal Wire wireGreen = new Wire("USB Green");
   publicfinal Wire wireBlack = new Wire("USB Black");
}
```

The USBPort, according to the USB specification, has four wires: 5V red, green, and white wires for data, and a black wire for ground, as shown in the following code:

```
interface PS2Device
{
  staticfinal String GND = "PS/2 GND";
  staticfinal String BLUE = "PS/2 Blue";
  staticfinal String BLACK = "PS/2 Black";
  staticfinal String GREEN = "PS/2 Green";
  staticfinal String WHITE = "PS/2 White";
  staticfinal String _5V = "PS/2 5V";
  public List<Wire> getWires();
  publicvoid printWiresConnectionsToRight();
}
class PS2Keyboard implements PS2Device
{
  publicfinal List<Wire> wires = Arrays.asList(
  new Wire(_5V),
  new Wire(WHITE),
  new Wire(GREEN),
  new Wire(BLACK),
  new Wire(BLUE),
  new Wire(GND));
  public List<Wire> getWires()
  {
    return Collections.unmodifiableList(wires);
  }
  publicvoid printWiresConnectionsToRight()
  {
    for(Wire wire : wires)
    wire.printWireConnectionsToRight();
  }
}
```

`PS2Keyboard` is the adapter. It's the old device that we need to use, as shown in the following code:

```
interface USBDevice
{
  publicvoid plugInto(USBPort port);
}
```

`USBDevice` is the target interface. It knows how to interface with a `USBPort`, as shown in the following code:

```
class PS2ToUSBAdapter implements USBDevice
{
  private PS2Device device;
  public PS2ToUSBAdapter(PS2Device device)
  {
    this.device = device;
  }
  publicvoid plugInto(USBPort port)
  {
    List<Wire> ps2wires = device.getWires();
    Wire wireRed = getWireWithNameFromList(PS2Device._5V,
    ps2wires);
    Wire wireWhite = getWireWithNameFromList(PS2Device.WHITE,
    ps2wires);
    Wire wireGreen = getWireWithNameFromList(PS2Device.GREEN,
    ps2wires);
    Wire wireBlack = getWireWithNameFromList(PS2Device.GND,
    ps2wires);
    port.wireRed.linkLeftTo(wireRed);
    port.wireWhite.linkLeftTo(wireWhite);
    port.wireGreen.linkLeftTo(wireGreen);
    port.wireBlack.linkLeftTo(wireBlack);
    device.printWiresConnectionsToRight();
  }
  private Wire getWireWithNameFromList(String name, List<Wire>
  ps2wires)
  {
    return ps2wires.stream()
    .filter(x -> name.equals(x.getName()))
    .findAny().orElse(null);
  }
}
```

`PS2ToUSBAdapter` is our adapter class. It knows how to do the wirings so that the old device can still be used by the new `USBPort`, as shown in the following code:

```
publicclass Main
{
  publicstaticvoid main (String[] args)
  {
    USBDevice adapter = new PS2ToUSBAdapter(new PS2Keyboard());
    adapter.plugInto(new USBPort());
  }
}
```

The output is as follows:

```
<terminated> Main (6) [Java Application] C:\Program Files\Java\jdk-9\bin\javaw.exe (Jul 24, 2017, 12:09:17 AM)
WireCap belonging to Wire PS/2 5V is linked to Wire USB Red5V
WireCap belonging to Wire PS/2 White is linked to Wire USB White
WireCap belonging to Wire PS/2 Green is linked to Wire USB Green
WireCap belonging to Wire PS/2 GND is linked to Wire USB Black
```

As expected, our device is wired to the USB port and ready to be used. All the wirings are done and, for example, if the USB port sets the red wire to 5 volts, that value reaches the keyboard, and if the keyboard sends data via the green wire, it will reach the USB port.

Proxy pattern

Whenever you work with Enterprise or Spring beans, mocked instances, and implement AOP, make RMI or JNI calls to another object with the same interface, or directly/indirectly use `java.lang.reflect.Proxy`, there is a proxy object involved. Its purpose is to provide a surrogate for a real object, with exactly the same footprint. It delegates the work to it while doing something else before or after the call. Types of proxy include the following:

- **Remote proxy**: This delegates the work to a remote object (different process, different machine), an Enterprise bean, for example. Wrapping existing non-Java old code (for example, C/C++) by using JNI, either manually or automatically (for example, by using SWIG to generate the glue code—see `http://www.swig.org/Doc1.3/Java.html#imclass`), is a form of a remote proxy pattern, since it uses a handle (pointer in C/C++) to access the actual object.
- **Protection proxy**: This does security/rights checks.
- **Cache proxy**: This uses memorization to speed up calls. One of the best examples is the Spring `@Cacheable` method, which caches the results of a method for the specific parameters and does not call the actual code, but returns from the cache the previously calculated result.
- **Virtual and smart proxies**. These add functionality to the method, such as logging performance metrics (creating an `@Aspect`, with an `@Pointcut` for the desired methods and defining an `@Around` advice) or doing lazy initialization.

The main difference between an adapter and a proxy is that the proxy provides exactly the same interface. The decorator pattern enhances the interface, while the adapter changes the interface.

Intent

The intent is to provide a surrogate for a real object in order to better control it. It is a handle to a real object that behaves like it, thus making the client code to use it just as it would use the real object.

Implementation

The following diagram models the proxy pattern. Notice that since both the real and the proxy subjects implement the same interface, they can be interchangeable:

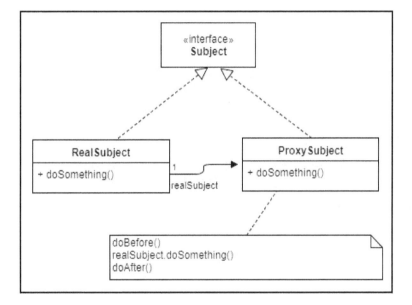

We can distinguish between the following actors in the implementation diagram:

- **Subject**: The existing interface used by the client
- **RealSubject**: The real object's class
- **ProxySubject**: The proxy class

Examples

The following code simulates a remote proxy that looks up a bean from the localhost EJB context. Our remote proxy is a geometry calculator running in another JVM. We will use a factory method to make both our proxy and real objects to demonstrate that they are interchangeable. The proxy version takes longer to compute, since we also simulate the JNI lookup part and send/retrieve the result. Take a look at the code:

```
package gof.structural.proxy;
publicclass Main
{
  publicstaticvoid main (String[] args) throws java.lang.Exception
  {
    GeometryCalculatorBean circle = GeometryCalculatorBeanFactory.
    REMOTE_PROXY.makeGeometryCalculator();
    System.out.printf("Circle diameter %fn",
    circle.calculateCircleCircumference(new Circle()));
  }
}
class Circle
{}
interface GeometryCalculatorBean
{
  publicdouble calculateCircleCircumference(Circle circle);
}
```

This is our subject, the interface that we want to implement. It simulates the modeling of both the @RemoteInterface and the @LocalInterface interfaces, as shown in the following code:

```
class GeometryBean implements GeometryCalculatorBean
{
  publicdouble calculateCircleCircumference(Circle circle)
  {
    return 0.1f;
  }
}
```

This is our real subject, the one that knows how to perform the actual geometry calculations, as shown in the following code:

```
class GeometryBeanProxy implements GeometryCalculatorBean
{
  private GeometryCalculatorBean bean;
  public GeometryBeanProxy() throws Exception
  {
    bean = doJNDILookup("remote://localhost:4447", "user",
    "password");
  }
  private GeometryCalculatorBean doJNDILookup
  (final String urlProvider, final String securityPrincipal, final
  String securityCredentials)
  throws Exception
  {
    System.out.println("Do JNDI lookup for bean");
    Thread.sleep(123);//simulate JNDI load for the remote location
    return GeometryCalculatorBeanFactory.LOCAL.
    makeGeometryCalculator();
  }
  publicdouble calculateCircleCircumference(Circle circle)
  {
    return bean.calculateCircleCircumference(circle);
  }
}
```

This is our proxy subject. Notice that it has no business logic; it delegates it to the real subject after it manages to establish a handle to it, as shown in the following code:

```
enum GeometryCalculatorBeanFactory
{
  LOCAL
  {
    public GeometryCalculatorBean makeGeometryCalculator()
    {
      returnnew GeometryBean();
    }
  },
  REMOTE_PROXY
  {
    public GeometryCalculatorBean makeGeometryCalculator()
    {
      try
      {
        returnnew GeometryBeanProxy();
      }
```

```
        catch (Exception e)
        {
          // TODO Auto-generated catch block
          e.printStackTrace();
        }
        returnnull;
      }
    };
    publicabstract GeometryCalculatorBean makeGeometryCalculator();
  }
```

The following output shows that the proxy manages to link to the real object and perform the required calculations:

```
<terminated> Main (1) [Java Application] C:\Program Files\Java\jdk-9\bin\javaw.exe (Jul 24, 2017, 12:10:13 AM)
Do JNDI lookup for bean
Circle diameter 0.100000
```

Decorator pattern

There are times when we need to add or remove functionality to/from existing code, without affecting it, and when it is not practical to make a subclass. The decorator comes in handy in these cases because it allows doing so without changing the existing code. It does this by implementing the same interface, aggregating the object that it is going to decorate, delegating all the common interface calls to it, and implementing in the child classes the new functionality. Apply this pattern to classes with a lightweight interface. In other cases, it is a better choice to extend the functionality by injecting the desired strategies into the component (strategy pattern). This will keep the changes local to a specific method, without the need to re-implement the other ones.

The decorated object and its decorator should be interchangeable. The decorator's interface must fully conform to the decorated object's interface.

Since it uses recursion, new functionality can be achieved by composing decorators. In this aspect, it resembles the composite pattern, which composes multiple objects with the intent to form complex structures that act as one. The decorator can be viewed as the piece of glass or the sheet of card from a passpartout (*a picture or photograph mounted between a piece of glass and a sheet of card*), where the picture/photograph itself is the decorated object. Strategy, on the other hand, can be viewed as the artist's signature on that picture/photograph.

The `JScrollPane` swing class is an example of a decorator because, it allows adding new functionalities, such as a scroll bar, around an existing container, and it can be done multiple times, as shown in this code:

```
JTextArea textArea = new JTextArea(10, 50);
JScrollPane scrollPane1 = new JScrollPane(textArea);
JScrollPane scrollPane2 = new JScrollPane(scrollPane1);
```

Intent

The intent is to dynamically extend the existing object's functionality without changing its code. It conforms to the original interface and is able to extend the functionally by using composition, rather than subclassing.

Implementation

The following diagram models the decorator pattern. It shows that the extended component and the decorated component can be replaced, one with the other. The decorator can be applied recursively; it can be applied to an existing component implementation but also applied to another decorator, or even to itself. The decorator interface is not fixed to the component interface; it can add extra methods, which may be used by the decorator's children, as shown in this diagram

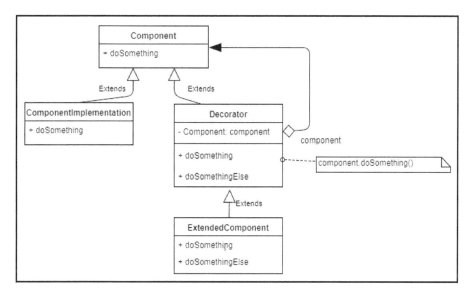

We can distinguish between the following actors in the implementation diagram:

- **Component**: This is the abstract component (it can be an interface)
- **ComponentImplementation**: This is one of the components we would like to decorate
- **Decorator**: This is an abstract component decorator
- **ExtendedComponent**: This is the component decorator that adds the extra functionality

Examples

The following code shows how a simple print ASCII text can be enhanced to print the hex equivalent string for the input, besides the actual text:

```
package gof.structural.decorator;
import java.util.stream.Collectors;
publicclass Main
{
  publicstaticvoid main (String[] args) throws java.lang.Exception
  {
    final String text = "text";
    final PrintText object = new PrintAsciiText();
    final PrintText printer = new PrintTextHexDecorator(object);
    object.print(text);
    printer.print(text);
  }
}
interface PrintText
{
  publicvoid print(String text);
}
PrintText is the component interface:
class PrintAsciiText implements PrintText
{
  publicvoid print(String text)
  {
    System.out.println("Print ASCII: " + text);
  }
}
```

`PrintASCIIText` is the component to be decorated. Notice that it knows only how to print `ASCII` text. We want to make it print in hexadecimal as well; we can do this using this code

```
class PrintTextHexDecorator implements PrintText
{
  private PrintText inner;
  public PrintTextHexDecorator(PrintText inner)
  {
    this.inner = inner;
  }
  publicvoid print(String text)
  {
    String hex = text.chars()
    .boxed()
    .map(x -> "0x" + Integer.toHexString(x))
    .collect(Collectors.joining(" "));
    inner.print(text + " -> HEX: " + hex);
  }
}
```

`PrintTextHexDecorator` is the decorator. It can be applied to other `PrintText` components as well. Let's say we want to implement a component `PrintToUpperText`. We may still use our existing decorator to make it print hex as well.

The following output displays the current functionality (ASCII) plus the newly added functionality (hexadecimal display):

```
<terminated> Main (2) [Java Application] C:\Program Files\Java\jdk-9\bin\javaw.exe (Jul 24, 2017, 4:30:07 PM)
Print ASCII: text
Print ASCII: text -> HEX: 0x74 0x65 0x78 0x74
```

Bridge pattern

During software design, we may face the problem that the same abstraction can have multiple implementations. This is mostly visible when doing cross-platform development. Examples could include a line-feed line break on Linux or the existence of a registry on Windows. A Java implementation that needs to get specific system information, by running specific OS calls, will definitely need to be able to vary the implementation. One way to do this is by using inheritance, but this will bind the children to a specific interface, which may not exist on different platforms.

In these cases, it is advisable to use the bridge pattern, since it allows moving away from a proliferation of classes that extend a specific abstraction to *nested generalizations*, a term coined by Rumbaugh, where we handle the first generalization, and then the other, thus multiplying all the combinations. This works fine if all subclasses are equally important and the same implementation methods are used by multiple interface objects. If, for some reason, a lot of code gets duplicated, this a sign that this pattern is not the right choice for the specific problem.

Intent

The intent is to decouple the abstraction from the implementation to allow them to vary independently. It does this by using inheritance, both in the public interface and in the implementation.

Implementation

The following diagram shows a possible bridge implementation. Notice that both the abstraction and the implementation can change, not only the interface but also the implementation code. For example, the refined abstraction could make use of the doImplementation3() that only the SpecificImplementation offers:

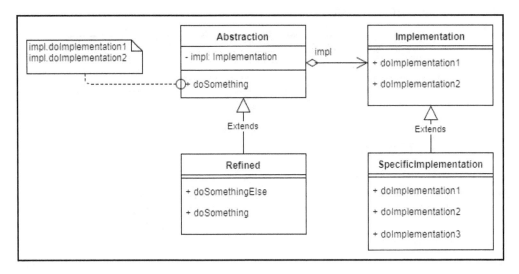

We can distinguish between the following actors in the implementation diagram:

- **Abstraction**: This is the abstract component
- **Implementation**: This is the abstract implementation
- **Refined**: This is the refined component
- **SpecificImplementation**: This is the concrete implementation

Examples

The following code presents an email client that makes use of an implementation based on the running platform. It can be enhanced with a factory method pattern to create the specific platform implementation:

```
package gof.structural.bridge;
publicclass Main
{
  publicstaticvoid main (String[] args)
  {
    new AllMessageClient(new WindowsImplementation())
    .sendMessageToAll("abc@gmail.com", "Test");
  }
}
interface PlatformBridge
{
  publicvoid forwardMessage(String msg);
}
```

PlatformBridge is our implementation abstraction class. It specifies what each implementation needs to offer —in our case, to forward a message given by text. Both the following implementations, Windows, and POSIX, know how to do the task:

```
class WindowsImplementation implements PlatformBridge
{
  publicvoid forwardMessage(String msg)
  {
    System.out.printf("Sending message n%s nFrom the windows
    machine", msg);
  }
}
class PosixImplementation implements PlatformBridge
{
  publicvoid forwardMessage(String msg)
  {
    System.out.printf("Sending message n%s nFrom the linux
```

```
      machine", msg);
   }
}
class MessageSender
{
   private PlatformBridge implementation;
   public MessageSender(PlatformBridge implementation)
   {
      this.implementation = implementation;
   }
   publicvoid sendMessage(String from, String to, String body)
   {
      implementation.forwardMessage(String.format("From :
      %s nTo : %s nBody : %s", from, to, body));
   }
}
```

The abstraction, `MessageSender`, sends a message using the platform-specific implementation. The `AllMessageClient` refined abstraction sends a message to a specific group—development_all@abc.com. Other possible refined abstractions could include platform-specific code and calls to the platform implementation. Here's the code:

```
class AllMessageClient extends MessageSender
{
   private String to = "development_all@abc.com";
   public MyMessageClient(PlatformBridge implementation)
   {
      super(implementation);
   }
   publicvoid sendMessageToAll(String from, String body)
   {
      sendMessage(from, to, body);
   }
}
```

The following output shows that all the message clients sent a message using the Windows implementation:

```
<terminated> Main (7) [Java Application] C:\Program Files\Java\jdk-9\bin\javaw.exe (Jul 24, 2017, 12:11:16 AM)
Sending message
From : abc@gmail.com
To : development_all@abc.com
Body : Test
From the windows machine
```

Composite pattern

The composite pattern, as the name suggests, is used when composing objects into a complex structure that acts as one (refer to the following diagram). Internally, it is using data structures, such as trees, graphs, arrays, or linked lists to represent the model:

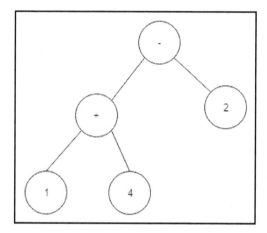

The JVM offers the best example of a composite pattern, since it is usually implemented as a stack machine (for portability reasons). Operations are pushed and popped from the current thread stack. For example, to calculate what *1 + 4 - 2* equals, it pushes 1, pushes 4, and executes add. The stack now has only value 5, pushes 2, and executes minus. Now the stack has only value 3, which is popped. The operation *1 + 4 + 2 -* (reversed polish notation) can be easily modeled using the composite pattern, where each node is either a value, complex value, or an operand. Each node has a perform method that performs the operation (push, execute, and pop or combine, depending on the type).

Composite makes use of recursive composition, where each part, leaf, or node is handled in the same manner by the client code.

Intent

The intent is to enable the modeling of objects into a tree or graph-like structures and treat them in the same manner. The client code does not need to know whether a node is an individual object (leaf node) or a composition of objects (a node with children, such as the root node); the client code can make an abstraction of these details and treat them uniformly.

Implementation

The following diagram shows that the client uses the component interface doSomething()
method. That method is implemented differently in root and leaf nodes. A root node can
have *1 to n* children; the leaf node has none. When the number of children is 2 and there are
no cycles, then we have the case of a binary tree:

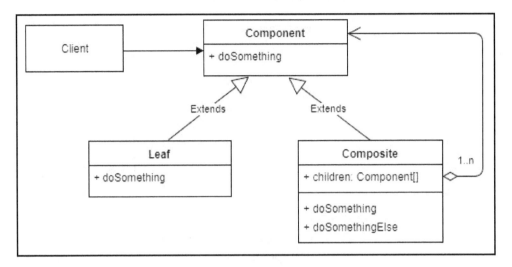

We can distinguish between the following actors in the implementation diagram:

- **Client**: The client code
- **Component**: The abstract node
- **Leaf**: The leaf node
- **Composite**: The composite node that has children that can be composite or leaf
  nodes

Examples

The following code models an arithmetic expression calculator. The expression is constructed as a composite and has only one method—getValue. This gives the current value; for leaf, it is the leaf numeric value, and for composite nodes, it is the children-composed value:

```
package gof.structural.composite;
publicclass Main
{
  publicstaticvoid main (String[] args) throws java.lang.Exception
  {
    ArithmeticComposite expr = new MinusOperand(
    new PlusOperand(new NumericValue(1), new NumericValue(4)),
    new NumericValue(2));
    System.out.printf("Value equals %dn", expr.getValue());
  }
}
```

The client code creates a *(1+4)-2* arithmetic expression and prints its value, as shown in the following code:

```
interface ArithmeticComposite
{
  publicint getValue();
}
```

ArithmeticComposite is our composite interface; it knows only how to return an integer value, which represents the value for the arithmetic expression (composition—ArithmeticOperand) or a hold value (leaf—NumericValue), as shown in the following code:

```
class NumericValue implements ArithmeticComposite
{
  privateint value;
  public NumericValue(int value)
  {
    this.value = value;
  }
  publicint getValue()
  {
    return value;
  }
}
abstractclass ArithmeticOperand implements ArithmeticComposite
{
```

```
      protected ArithmethicComposite left;
      protected ArithmethicComposite right;
      public ArithmethicOperand(ArithmeticComposite left,
      ArithmeticComposite right)
      {
        this.left = left;
        this.right = right;
      }
  }
  class PlusOperand extends ArithmeticOperand
  {
      public PlusOperand(ArithmeticComposite left,
      ArithmeticComposite right)
      {
        super(left, right);
      }
      publicint getValue()
      {
        return left.getValue() + right.getValue();
      }
  }
  class MinusOperand extends ArithmeticOperand
  {
      public MinusOperand(ArithmeticComposite left,
      ArithmeticComposite right)
      {
        super(left, right);
      }
      publicint getValue()
      {
        return left.getValue() - right.getValue();
      }
  }
```

PlusOperand and MinusOperand are the current supported arithmetic types. They know how to represent a plus (+) and minus (-) arithmetic expression.

As expected, a *(1+4)-2* arithmetic expression returns 3 and the values get printed to the console, as shown in the following screenshot:

```
<terminated> Main (4) [Java Application] C:\Program Files\Java\jdk-9\bin\javaw.exe (Jul 24, 2017, 12:29:33 AM)
Value equals 3
```

Façade pattern

Many complex systems are reducible to just a couple of their use cases, exposed by the subsystems. By doing so, the client code does not need to know about the internals of the subsystem. In other words, the client code is decoupled from it and it takes less time for the developer to use it. This is known as a façade pattern, where the façade object is responsible for exposing all the subsystem's functionality. This concept resembles encapsulation, where we hide the internals of an object. With façade, we hide the internals of a subsystem and expose just the essentials. The consequence is that the user is limited to the functionality exposed by the façade, and is not able to use/reuse specific functionality from the subsystem.

The façade pattern needs to adopt the internal subsystem interface (many interfaces) to the client code interface (one interface). It does this by creating a new interface, while the adapter pattern adapts to and from existing interfaces (sometimes more than one old class is needed to provide the desired functionality to the new code). The façade does for structures what the mediator does for object communication—it unifies and simplifies usage. In the first case, the client code accesses a subsystem's functionality by using the façade object; in the second case, objects that are not aware of one another (loose coupled) can interact by using a mediator/facilitator.

Intent

The intent is to provide a single unified interface for a complex subsystem. This simplifies the usage of big and complex systems by providing the interface for the most important use cases.

Implementation

The following diagram shows how a subsystem's usage can be simplified and decoupled from the client code. The façade is the entry point to the subsystem; therefore, the subsystem code can easily be switched to a different implementation. The client dependencies can also be managed more easily and are more visible:

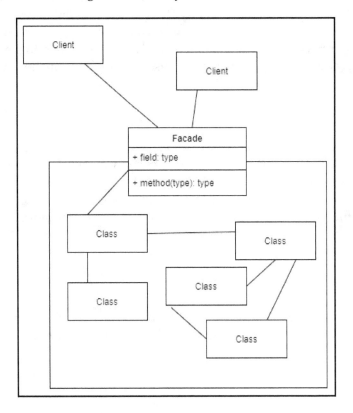

We can distinguish the following actors in the implementation diagram:

- **Client**: The subsystem client code
- **Façade**: The subsystem interface
- **Subsystem**: The classes defined in the subsystem

Examples

Coffee machines are like façades for the coffee grinders and coffee brewers, because they hide their functionalities. The following code simulates a coffee machine that grinds coffee beans, brews the coffee, and places it in a coffee cup.

The issue, as you will find out from the following code, is that we cannot get fine-sized ground coffee (we have to grind the beans a little longer), since the `serveCoffee()` method knows only how to make coarse-sized ground coffee. This could be fine for some coffee drinkers but not for all:

```
package gof.structural.facade;
publicclass Main
{
  publicstaticvoid main (String[] args) throws java.lang.Exception
  {
    CoffeeMachineFacade facade = new SuperstarCoffeeMachine();
    facade.serveCoffee();
  }
}
class GroundCoffee
{}
class Water
{}
class CoffeeCup
{}
```

`GroundCoffee`, `Water`, and `CoffeeCup` are the item classes that we are going to use:

```
interface CoffeeMachineFacade
{
  public CoffeeCup serveCoffee() throws Exception;
}
```

`CoffeeMachineFacade` is our façade. It offers a single method that returns a `CoffeCup` containing `Coffee`:

```
interface CoffeeGrinder
{
  publicvoid startGrinding();
  public GroundCoffee stopGrinding();
}
interface CoffeeMaker
{
  publicvoid pourWater(Water water);
  publicvoid placeCup(CoffeeCup cup);
```

```
  publicvoid startBrewing(GroundCoffee groundCoffee);
  public CoffeeCup finishBrewing();
}
class SuperstarCoffeeGrinder implements CoffeeGrinder
{
  publicvoid startGrinding()
  {
    System.out.println("Grinding...");
  }
  public GroundCoffee stopGrinding ()
  {
    System.out.println("Done grinding");
    returnnew GroundCoffee();
  }
}
class SuperstarCoffeeMaker implements CoffeeMaker
{
  public CoffeeCup finishBrewing()
  {
    System.out.println("Done brewing. Enjoy!");
    returnnull;
  }
  @Override
  publicvoid pourWater(Water water)
  {
    System.out.println("Pouring water...");
  }
  @Override
  publicvoid placeCup(CoffeeCup cup)
  {
    System.out.println("Placing the cup...");
  }
  @Override
  publicvoid startBrewing(GroundCoffee groundCoffee)
  {
    System.out.println("Brewing...");
  }
}
```

To make a coffee, we use different machines, such as a coffee grinder and a coffee maker. They are all Superstar Inc. products. The façade machine is a virtual machine; it's just an interface to our existing machines and knows how to make use of them. Unfortunately, it isn't highly configurable, but it gets the job done for most of the existing coffee drinkers. Let's look at this code:

```
class SuperstarCoffeeMachine implements CoffeeMachineFacade
{
  public CoffeeCup serveCoffee() throws InterruptedException
  {
    CoffeeGrinder grinder = new SuperstarCoffeeGrinder();
    CoffeeMaker brewer = new SuperstarCoffeeMaker();
    CoffeeCup cup = new CoffeeCup();
    grinder.startGrinding();
    Thread.sleep(500);//wait for grind size coarse
    brewer.placeCup(cup);
    brewer.pourWater(new Water());
    brewer.startBrewing(grinder.stopGrinding());
    Thread.sleep(1000);//wait for the brewing process
    return brewer.finishBrewing();
  }
}
```

The following output shows that our façade managed to serve our morning coffee:

```
<terminated> Main (3) [Java Application] C:\Program Files\Java\jdk-9\bin\javaw.exe (Jul 24, 2017, 8:10:08 AM)
Grinding...
Placing the cup...
Pouring water...
Done grinding
Brewing...
Done brewing. Enjoy!
```

Flyweight pattern

Creating objects costs time and resources. The best examples are Java constant string creation, `Boolean.valueOf(boolean b)`, or `Character valueOf(char c)`, since they never create instances; they return immutable cached instances. To speed up (and keep the memory footprint low), applications use object pools. The difference between the object pool pattern and the flyweight pattern is that the first (creation pattern) is a container that keeps mutable domain objects, while the flyweight (structure pattern) is an immutable domain object. Since they're immutable, their internal state is set on creation, and the extrinsic state is given from outside on each method call.

Most web applications use connection pools—a database connection is created/obtained, used, and sent back to the pool. Since this pattern is so common, it has a name: Connection Flyweight (see `http://wiki.c2.com/?ConnectionFlyweight`). Other resources, such as sockets or threads (thread pool pattern), also make use of object pools.

The difference between flyweight and façade is that the first knows how to make many small objects, while the latter makes a single object that simplifies and hides the complexity of a subsystem, made of many objects.

Intent

The intent is to reduce memory footprint by sharing state among similar objects. It can be done only if the huge number of objects can be reduced to a few that are representative, that do not rely on object equality, and their state can be externalized.

Implementation

The following diagram shows that the flyweight object is returned from the pool and, to function, it needs the external state (extrinsic) passed as an argument. Some flyweights can share state with others, but this is not an enforced rule:

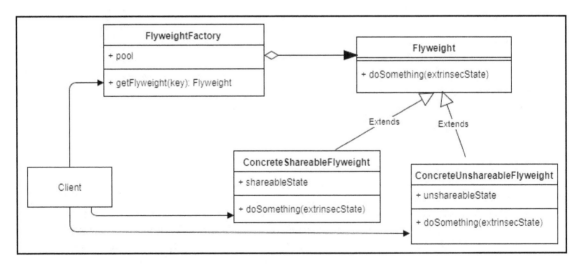

We can distinguish the following actors in the implementation diagram:

- **Client**: The client code.
- **FlyweightFactory**: This creates flyweights if they do not exist, and returns them from the pool if they exist.
- **Flyweight**: The abstract flyweight.
- **ConcreateShareableFlyweight**: The flyweight designed to be have a shared state with its peers.
- **ConcreateUnshareableFlyweight**: The flyweight that does not share its state. It could be composed from multiple concrete flyweights—for example, a structure made out of 3D cubes and spheres.

Examples

The following code simulates a 3D world with an attached physics engine. Since creating new 3D objects is heavy and costly in terms of memory, once created they will be the same and just moved from one place to another. Imagine a 3D world with a lot of rocks, trees, bushes, and different textures. By having only one rock of a kind, a tree, bush (they could share some textures) and just remembering where they are located, we save a lot of memory and we are still able to fill with them a considerable large-sized terrain:

```java
package gof.structural.flyweight;
import java.util.ArrayList;
import java.util.List;
import java.util.Map;
import java.util.concurrent.ConcurrentHashMap;
import java.util.stream.Collectors;
publicclass Main
{
  publicstaticvoid main (String[] args) throws java.lang.Exception
  {
    World world = new World();
    world.get3DObject(_3DObjectTypes.Cube).makeVisible().
    move(10d, -13.3d, 90.0d);
    world.get3DObject(_3DObjectTypes.Sphere).makeVisible().
    move(11d, -12.9d, 90.0d);
    world.get3DObject(_3DObjectTypes.Cube).makeVisible().
    move(9d, -12.9d, 90.0d);
  }
}
enum _3DObjectTypes
{
  Cube,
```

```
   Sphere
}
```

Our 3D world is currently constructed only from cubes and spheres. They can be grouped together to form more complex forms, as shown in the following code:

```java
class PhysicsEngine
{
  publicvoid animateCollision(_3DObject collider, _3DObject
  collidee)
  {
    System.out.println("Animate Collision between " + collider +
    " and " + collidee);
  }
}
class World
{
  private PhysicsEngine engine = new PhysicsEngine();
  private Map<String, _3DObject> objects = new ConcurrentHashMap<>();
  private Map<String, Location> locations = new ConcurrentHashMap<>();
  public _3DObject get3DObject(_3DObjectTypes type)
  {
    String name = type.toString();
    if (objects.containsKey(name))
    return objects.get(name);
    _3DObject obj = make3DObject(type);
    objects.put(obj.getName(), obj);
    return obj;
  }
  private _3DObject make3DObject(_3DObjectTypes type)
  {
    switch (type)
    {
      caseCube:
      returnnew Cube(this, type.toString());
      caseSphere:
      returnnew Sphere(this, type.toString());
      default:
      returnnew _3DObject(this, type.toString());
    }
  }
  publicvoid move(_3DObject obj, Location location)
  {
    final List<String> nearObjectNames = getNearObjects(location);
    locations.put(obj.getName(), location);
    for (String nearObjectName: nearObjectNames)
    {
      engine.animateCollision(objects.get(nearObjectName), obj);
```

```
      }
   }
   private List<String> getNearObjects(Location location)
   {
      if (objects.size() < 2)
      returnnew ArrayList<>();
      return objects.values().stream()
      .filter(obj ->
      {
         Location loc = locations.get(obj.getName());
         return loc != null && loc.isNear(location, 1);
      })
      .map(obj -> obj.getName())
      .collect(Collectors.toList());
   }
}
```

The World class represents the flyweight factory. It knows how to construct them and pass itself as and extrinsic state. The World class, besides the rendering part, makes use of the expensive physics engine that knows how to model collisions. Let's see the code:

```
class _3DObject
{
   private World world;
   private String name;
   public _3DObject(World world, String name)
   {
      this.world = world;
      this.name = name;
   }
   public String getName()
   {
      return name;
   }
   @Override
   public String toString()
   {
      return name;
   }
   public _3DObject makeVisible()
   {
      returnthis;
   }
   publicvoid move(double x, double y, double z)
   {
      System.out.println("Moving object " + name + " in the world");
      world.move(this, new Location(x, y, z));
```

```
     }
  }
  class Cube extends _3DObject
  {
     public Cube(World world, String name)
     {
        super(world, name);
     }
  }
  class Sphere extends _3DObject
  {
     public Sphere(World world, String name)
     {
        super(world, name);
     }
  }
```

The 3D objects, `Sphere` and `Cube`, are the flyweights, they do not have an identity. The `World` class knows their identity and attributes (location, color, texture, and size). Take a look at this code:

```
  class Location
  {
     public Location(double x, double y, double z)
     {
        super();
     }
     publicboolean isNear(Location location, int radius)
     {
        returntrue;
     }
  }
```

The following output shows that even if there was already a cube in the 3D world, adding another will make it collide with the existing objects—another cube and a sphere. None of them have identity; they are all representatives of their type:

```
<terminated> Main (5) [Java Application] C:\Program Files\Java\jdk-9\bin\javaw.exe (Jul 24, 2017, 11:21:08 PM)
Moving object Cube in the world
Moving object Sphere in the world
Animate Collision between Cube and Sphere
Moving object Cube in the world
Animate Collision between Sphere and Cube
Animate Collision between Cube and Cube
```

Summary

In this chapter, we learned about the GOF structural patterns. We looked at their descriptions and intent and illustrated their use with sample code. We learned why, when, and how to apply them, and also looked at the subtle differences between them. We also briefly covered other less known structural patterns.

In the following chapters, we will see how some of these patterns change in the functional and reactive world.

5
Functional Patterns

The objective of this chapter is to learn about functional patterns and the changes to the traditional patterns added by the introduction of a functional style of programming that is now possible in the most important programming languages. Java 8 brought in functional features that added a new level of abstraction, affecting the way we write some of the object-oriented design patterns, even making some of them irrelevant. In this chapter, we will see how design patterns are changed, or even replaced, by the new language features. In his paper, *Design Patterns in Dynamic Languages*, Peter Norvig noticed that 16 out of the 23 design patterns are simpler or replaced by existing language features in dynamic languages, such as Dylan. The full paper is available at `http://norvig.com/design-patterns/`. In this chapter, we are going to see what can be replaced, and how and what the new emerged patterns are. As Peter Norvig said in his paper, *Long ago, subroutine call was just a pattern*, as languages evolve, expect the patterns to change or be replaced.

To run the code from this chapter, we used the jshell REPL utility available in Java and accessible from `$JAVA_HOME/bin/jshell` on Linux or `%JAVA_HOME%/bin/jshell.exe` in Windows.

Introducing functional programming

During the 1930s, the mathematician Alonzo Church developed lambda calculus. This was the starting point for the functional programming paradigm, since it provided the theoretical grounds. The next step was the design of **LISP** (short for **List Programming**) in 1958, by John McCarthy. LISP is the first functional programming language, and some of its flavors, such as Common LISP, are still used today.

In functional programming (often abbreviated to FP), functions are first-class citizens; this means that software is built by composing functions, rather than objects, as OOP. This is done in a declarative way, *Tell don't ask*, by composing functions, promoting immutability, and avoiding the side effects and shared data. This leads to a more concise code that is resilient to changes, predictable, and easier to maintain and read by business people.

Functional code has a higher signal-to-noise ratio; we have to write less code to achieve the same thing as in OOP. By avoiding side effects and data mutations, and relying on data transformation, the system becomes much simpler, and easier to debug and fix. Another benefit is the predictability. We know that the same function for the same input will always give the same output; therefore, it can also be used in parallel computation, called before or after any other function (the CPU/compiler does not need to make assumptions on the call order) and its return value can be cached once calculated, thus improving performance.

Being a declarative type of programming, it focuses more on what needs to be done, in contrast to the imperative style, where the focus is on how it should be done. A sample flow can be seen in the following diagram:

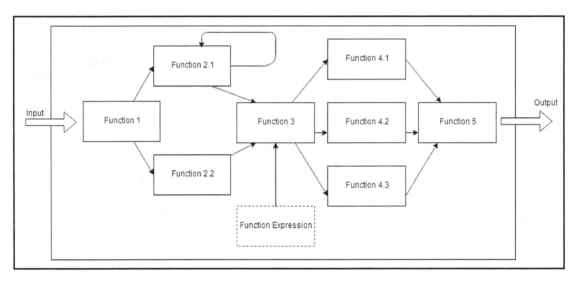

The functional programming paradigm uses the following concepts and principles:

- Lambda expressions
- Pure functions
- Referential transparency
- First-class functions
- Higher-order functions
- Function composition
- Currying
- Closure
- Immutability

- Functors
- Applicatives
- Monads

Lambda expressions

The name comes from lambda calculus, where the Greek letter lambda (λ) is used to bind a term to a function. The lambda terms are either variables (x, for example), abstractions—such as $\lambda.x.M$, where M is the function—or applications, where two terms, M and N, are applied one to another. With the constructed (composed) terms, it is now possible to do expression reduction and/or conversion. Lambda-expression reduction can be tested online by using interpreters, such as the one available at Berkeley: `https://people.eecs.berkeley.edu/~gongliang13/lambda/`.

The following is an example of a lambda-calculus lambda expression for calculating the circle radius square when the x, y coordinates are known:

$$(x, y) \rightarrow x^2 + y^2$$

It is mathematically defined an n-ary function:

$$\lambda xy.x * x + y * y$$

The application is as follows:

$$\left((x, y) \rightarrow x^2 + y^2\right)(1, 2) = 5$$

Here is the curried version (notice the extra reduction step):

$$\left(\left((x, y) \rightarrow x^2 + y^2\right)(1)\right)(2) = 5$$

The main benefit of using lambda expressions over statements is that lambda expressions can be composed and reduced to simpler forms.

Java 8 introduced lambda expressions (made available before by using anonymous classes) and the implementation makes use of the invoke dynamic introduced in Java 7, instead of anonymous classes for performance (too many generated classes that need to be loaded) and customization (future changes) reasons.

Pure functions

A pure function is a function that has no side effects and its output is the same for the same input (predictable and cacheable). A side effect is an action that modifies the outside context of the function. Examples of this include to the following:

- Writing to a file/console/network/screen
- Modifying an outside variable/state
- Calling a non-pure function
- Starting a process

Side effects are sometimes unavoidable or even desirable—I/O or low-level operations are examples of code with side effects (von Neumann machines work because of side effects). As a rule of thumb, try to isolate the functions with side effects from the rest of the code. Haskell and other functional programming languages use monads for the task. We will have an introductory section on monads later.

Since the output of a pure function is predictable, it can also be replaced with the cached output; this is why pure functions are said to provide referential transparency. Pure functions are easier to read and understand—in his book, *Clean Code*, Robert Martin writes:

> "Indeed, the ratio of time spent reading versus writing is well over 10 to 1. We are constantly reading old code as part of the effort to write new code. ...[Therefore,] making it easy to read makes it easier to write."

Favoring pure functions in the code enhances productivity and allows newcomers to spend less time reading the new code and more time using and fixing it.

Referential transparency

Referential transparency is the property of a function to be replaceable with its return value for the input. The benefits are tremendous, since this favors memorization (caching of the return value) and parallelization of the call to the specific function. Testing such a function is also easy.

First-class functions

First-class functions are functions that can be treated much like the objects from the object-oriented programming—created, stored, used as parameters, and returned as values.

Higher-order functions

Higher-order functions are functions that can take other functions as parameters, create, and return them. They promote code reuse by making use of existing and already-tested small functions. For example, in the following code, we calculate the average in Celsius for the given temperatures in Fahrenheit:

```
jshell> IntStream.of(70, 75, 80, 90).map(x -> (x - 32)*5/9).average();
$4 ==> OptionalDouble[25.5]
```

Notice the use of the lambda expression inside the higher-order map function. The same lambda expression can be utilized in multiple places to convert temperatures.

```
jshell> IntUnaryOperator convF2C = x -> (x-32)*5/9;
convF2C ==> $Lambda$27/1938056729@4bec1f0c
jshell> IntStream.of(70, 75, 80, 90).map(convF2C).average();
$6 ==> OptionalDouble[25.5]
jshell> convF2C.applyAsInt(80);
$7 ==> 26Function
```

Composition

In mathematics, functions are composed/chained together by using the output of a function as the input of the next. The same rule applies in functional programming, where first-class functions are used by higher-order functions. The preceding code already contains such an example—see the use of the convF2C pure function inside the map function.

To make the function composition more visible, we may rewrite the conversion formula by making use of the andThen method:

```
jshell> IntUnaryOperator convF2C = ((IntUnaryOperator)(x ->
x-32)).andThen(x -> x *5).andThen(x -> x / 9);
convF2C ==>
java.util.function.IntUnaryOperator$$Lambda$29/1234776885@dc24521
jshell> convF2C.applyAsInt(80);
$23 ==> 26
```

Currying

Currying is a process used to transform an n-ary function into a series or unary functions, and it was named after Haskell Curry, an American mathematician. The form $g :: x \to y \to z$ is the curried form of $f :: (x, y) \to z$. For the square radius presented formula earlier, $f(x, y) = x^2 + y^2$, a curried version, without the use of BiFunction, would use apply multiple times. A single application of a function would just replace the parameter with a value, as we saw earlier. The following code shows how to curry a two-parameter function, for *n* parameters there will be n calls to the `Function<X, Y>` class's apply function:

```
jshell> Function<Integer, Function<Integer, Integer>> square_radius = x ->
y -> x*x + y*y;
square_radius ==> $Lambda$46/1050349584@6c3708b3
jshell> List<Integer> squares = Arrays.asList(new Tuple<Integer,
Integer>(1, 5), new Tuple<Integer, Integer>(2, 3)).stream().
map(a -> square_radius.apply(a.y).apply(a.x)).
collect(Collectors.toList());
squares ==> [26, 13]
```

Closure

Closure is a technique to implement lexical scoping. Lexical scoping allows us to access the outer context variables inside the inner scope. Imagine that in our previous example the *y* variable had already been assigned a value. The lambda expression could remain a unary expression and still use the *y* as a variable. This could lead to some very hard-to-find bugs, as in the following code, where we would expect that the return value of our function remains the same. The closure captures the current value of an object, as we can see in the following code, where our expectation is that the `add100` function will always add 100 to the given input, but it does not:

```
jshell> Integer a = 100
a ==> 100
jshell> Function<Integer, Integer> add100 = b -> b + a;
add100 ==> $Lambda$49/553871028@eec5a4a
jshell> add100.apply(9);
$38 ==> 109
jshell> a = 101;
a ==> 101
jshell> add100.apply(9);
$40 ==> 110
```

Here, we would expect to get 109, but it replies with 110, which is correct (101 plus 9 equals 110); our *a* variable changed from 100 to 101. Closures need to be used with precaution, and, as a rule of thumb, use the final keyword to limit the changes. Closures are not always evil; they can be handy in cases where we want to share the current state (and be able to modify it whenever needed). For example, we would use closure in an API that requires a callback providing a database connection (abstract connection); we would use different closures, each one providing a connection based on some specific database-provider settings, usually read from a properties file known in the outer context. It can be used to implement the template pattern in a functional way.

Immutability

In *Effective Java*, Joshua Bloch offered the following advice: "*Treat objects as immutable.*" The reason this advice needs to be taken into consideration in the OOP world lies in the fact that mutable code has many moving parts; it is too complex to be easily understood and fixed. Promoting immutability simplifies the code and allows developers to focus on the flow instead—not on the side effects that a piece of code could have. The worst side effects are the ones where a small change in one place can produce catastrophic results in another (Butterfly effect). A mutable code can sometimes be hard to parallelize and often resorts to different locks.

Functors

Functors allow us to apply functions to the given containers. They know how to unwrap the value from the wrapped object, apply the given function, and return another functor containing the resulted/transformed wrapped object. They are useful because they abstract multiple idioms, such as collections, futures (promises), and Optionals. The following code demonstrates the use of the Optional functor from Java, where Optional could be a given value as a result of applying a function to an existing wrapped value (Optional of 5):

```
jshell> Optional<Integer> a = Optional.of(5);
a ==> Optional[5]
```

Now we apply the function to the wrapped integer object with value of 5 and we get a new; optional holding value of 4.5:

```
jshell> Optional<Float> b = a.map(x -> x * 0.9f);
b ==> Optional[4.5]
jshell> b.get()
$7 ==> 4.5
```

Optional is a functor similar to Maybe (Just | Nothing) from Haskell—it even has a static Optional.empty() method that returns an optional with no value (nothing).

Applicatives

Applicatives add a new level of wrapping—instead of applying a function to a wrapped object, the function is wrapped too. In the following code, the function is wrapped in an optional. To prove one of the applicatives' usages, we also provide an identity (everything remains the same) optional in case the desired function (toUpperCase in our case) is empty. Since there is no syntax sugar to automatically apply a wrapped function, we need to do that manually—see the get().apply() code. Notice the usage of the Java 9 added method Optional.or(), which returns another Optional lazily, in case our input Optional is empty:

```
jshell> Optional<String> a = Optional.of("Hello Applicatives")
a ==> Optional[Hello Applicatives]
jshell> Optional<Function<String, String>> upper =
Optional.of(String::toUpperCase)
upper ==> Optional[$Lambda$14/2009787198@1e88b3c]
jshell> a.map(x -> upper.get().apply(x))
$3 ==> Optional[HELLO APPLICATIVES]
```

This is our applicative that knows how to uppercase the given string. Let's see the code:

```
jshell> Optional<Function<String, String>> identity =
Optional.of(Function.identity())
identity ==>
Optional[java.util.function.Function$$Lambda$16/1580893732@5c3bd550]
jshell> Optional<Function<String, String>> upper = Optional.empty()
upper ==> Optional.empty
jshell> a.map(x -> upper.or(() -> identity).get().apply(x))
$6 ==> Optional[Hello Applicatives]
```

The preceding code is our applicative that applies the identity function (output is the same as input) to the given string.

Monads

A **monad** applies a function that returns a wrapped value to a wrapped value. Java contains examples such as `Stream`, `CompletableFuture`, and the already-presented `Optional`. The `flatMap` function does this by applying the given function, as the following code demonstrates, to a list of ZIP codes that may or may not exist in a ZIP code map:

```
jshell> Map<Integer, String> codesMapping = Map.of(400500, "Cluj-Napoca",
75001, "Paris", 10115, "Berlin", 10000, "New York")
codesMapping ==> {400500=Cluj-Napoca, 10115=Berlin, 10000=New York,
75001=Paris}
jshell> List<Integer> codes = List.of(400501, 75001, 10115, 10000)
codes ==> [400501, 75001, 10115, 10000]
jshell> codes.stream().flatMap(x -> Stream.ofNullable(codesMapping.get(x)))
$3 ==> java.util.stream.ReferencePipeline$7@343f4d3d
jshell> codes.stream().flatMap(x ->
Stream.ofNullable(codesMapping.get(x))).collect(Collectors.toList());
$4 ==> [Paris, Berlin, New York]
```

Haskell makes use of the following monads (imported in other functional programming languages). They are also important for the Java world because of their powerful concepts of abstraction (see `https://wiki.haskell.org/All_About_Monads`):

- The reader monad allows sharing and reading from an environment state. It provides edge capabilities between the mutable part and the immutable part of a software.
- The writer monad is used for appending state to multiple writers—much like the logging process that logs to multiple writers (console/file/network).
- The state monad is a reader and a writer at the same time.

To grasp the concepts of the functor, applicatives, and monads, we recommend checking out `http://adit.io/posts/2013-04-17-functors,_applicatives,_and_monads_in_pictures.html` and `https://bartoszmilewski.com/2011/01/09/monads-for-the-curious-programmer-part-1/`. There are also some great collections of functional goodies available in the cyclops-react library at `https://github.com/aol/cyclops-react`.

Introducing functional programming in Java

Functional programming is based on Streams and Lambda expressions, both introduced in Java 8. Libraries such as Retrolambda allow Java 8 code to run on older JVM runtimes, such as Java 5,6, or 7 (typically used for Android development).

Lambda expressions

Lambda expressions are syntax sugar for the use of the `java.util.functions` package interfaces. The most important ones are the following:

- `BiConsumer<T,U>`: An operation that consumes two input arguments and returns no result, usually used in the maps `forEach` method. It has support for chaining `BiConsumers` by using the `andThen` method.

- `BiFunction<T,U,R>`: A function that accepts two arguments and produces a result, used by calling its `apply` method.

- `BinaryOperator<T>`: An operation upon two operands of the same type, producing a result of the same type as the operands, used by calling its inherited `apply` method. It statically offers the `minBy` and `maxBy` methods, which return the lesser/greater of the two elements.

- `BiPredicate<T,U>`: A Boolean return function of two arguments (also called predicates), used by calling its `test` method.

- `Consumer<T>`: An operation that consumes a single input argument. Just like its binary counterpart, it supports chaining and is applied by calling its `apply` method, as in the following example, where the consumer is the `System.out.println` method:

```
jshell> Consumer<Integer> printToConsole = System.out::println;
print ==> $Lambda$24/117244645@5bcab519
jshell> printToConsole.accept(9)
9
```

- `Function<T,R>`: A function that accepts one argument and produces a result. It transforms the input, not mutate. It can be used directly by calling its apply method, chained using `andThen` and composed by using the `compose` method, as shown in the following sample code. This allows our code to stay **DRY** (short for **Don't Repeat Yourself**) by composing new functions out of existing ones:

```
jshell> Function<Integer, Integer> square = x -> x*x;
square ==> $Lambda$14/1870647526@47c62251
jshell> Function<Integer, String> toString = x -> "Number : " +
x.toString();
toString ==> $Lambda$15/1722023916@77caeb3e
jshell> toString.compose(square).apply(4);
$3 ==> "Number : 16"
jshell> square.andThen(toString).apply(4);
$4 ==> "Number : 16"
```

- `Predicate<T>`: A Boolean return function of one argument. In the following code, we are going to test whether a string is completely lowercase:

```
jshell> Predicate<String> isLower = x -> x.equals(x.toLowerCase())
isLower ==> $Lambda$25/507084503@490ab905
jshell> isLower.test("lower")
$8 ==> true
jshell> isLower.test("Lower")
$9 ==> false
```

- `Supplier<T>`: This is a supplier of values:

```
jshell> String lambda = "Hello Lambda"
lambda ==> "Hello Lambda"
jshell> Supplier<String> closure = () -> lambda
closure ==> $Lambda$27/13329486@13805618
jshell> closure.get()
$13 ==> "Hello Lambda"
```

- `UnaryOperator<T>`: A specialized function that acts on a single operand that produces a result of the same type as its operand; it can be replaced with `Function<T, T>`.

Streams

Streams are a pipeline of functions that transform, instead of mutating, data. They have creators, intermediate, and terminal operations. To obtain values out of the stream, the terminal operations need to be called. Streams are not data structures, and they cannot be reused, once consumed it remains closed—if collected a second time, `java.lang.IllegalStateException` exception: stream has already been operated upon or closed will be thrown.

Stream creator operations

Streams can be sequential or parallel. They can be created from the `Collection` interface, JarFile, ZipFile, or BitSet, and, starting from Java 9, from the `Optional class stream()` method. The `Collection` class supports the `parallelStream()` method, which may return a parallel stream or a serial stream. It is possible to construct streams of various types, such as boxed primitives (Integer, Long, Double) or other classes, by calling the appropriate `Arrays.stream(...)`. The result of calling it for a primitive type is a specialized Stream of the following: `IntStream`, `LongStream`, or `DoubleStream`. Those specialized stream classes can construct streams by using one of their static methods, such as `generate(...)`, `of(...)`, `empty()`, `iterate(...)`, `concat(...)`, `range(...)`, `rangeClosed(...)`, or `builder()`. Getting a stream of data from a `BufferedReader` object can be easily done by calling the `lines(...)` method, also present in a static form in the `Files` class, where it is used to get all the lines from a file given by Path. The `Files` class provides other stream creator methods, such as `list(...)`, `walk(...)`, and `find(...)`.

Java 9 added more classes that return streams besides the already mentioned `Optional`, such as the `Matcher` class (the `results(...)` method) or the `Scanner` class (the `findAll(...)` and `tokens()` methods).

Stream intermediate operations

The intermediate stream operations are applied lazily; this means that the actual call is done only after the terminal operation gets called. In the following code, using names randomly generated online using `http://www.behindthename.com/random/?`, the search will stop once the first valid name is found (it just returns a `Stream<String>` object):

```
jshell> Stream<String> stream = Arrays.stream(new String[] {"Benny
Gandalf", "Aeliana Taina","Sukhbir Purnima"}).
...> map(x -> { System.out.println("Map " + x); return x; }).
...> filter(x -> x.contains("Aeliana"));
stream ==> java.util.stream.ReferencePipeline$2@6eebc39e
jshell> stream.findFirst();
Map Benny Gandalf
Map Aeliana Taina
$3 ==> Optional[Aeliana Taina]
```

Stream intermediate operations contain operations such as these:

- `sequential()`: Sets the current stream as a serial stream.
- `parallel()`: Sets the current stream as possibly parallel stream. As a rule of thumb, use parallel streams for large data sets where parallelization adds a performance boost. In our code, doing the operations in parallel will lead to a performance decrease, since the cost of parallelization is bigger than the gain, plus we are processing some entries that otherwise won't get processed:

```
jshell> Stream<String> stream = Arrays.stream(new String[] {"Benny
Gandalf", "Aeliana Taina","Sukhbir Purnima"}).
...> parallel().
...> map(x -> { System.out.println("Map " + x); return x; }).
...> filter(x -> x.contains("Aeliana"));
stream ==> java.util.stream.ReferencePipeline$2@60c6f5b
jshell> stream.findFirst();
Map Benny Gandalf
Map Aeliana Taina
Map Sukhbir Purnima
$14 ==> Optional[Aeliana Taina]
```

- `unordered()`: Processes the input in an unordered fashion. It makes the output order indeterministic for sequence streams and can lead to performance improvements for the parallel execution by allowing some aggregate functions, such as distinct or `groupBy` to be implemented more efficiently.
- `onClose(..)`: Closes resources used by the stream using the given input handler. The `Files.lines(...)` stream makes use of it to close the input file, such as in the following code, where it is automatically closed, but the stream can also be manually closed by calling the `close()` method:

```
jshell> try (Stream<String> stream =
Files.lines(Paths.get("d:/input.txt"))) {
...> stream.forEach(System.out::println);
...> }
Benny Gandalf
Aeliana Taina
Sukhbir Purnima
```

- `filter(..)`: Filters the input by applying a predicate.
- `map(..)`: Transforms the input by applying a function.
- `flatMap(..)`: Replaces the input with the values from a stream based on a mapping function.
- `distinct()`: Uses `Object.equals()` to return distinct values.

- `sorted(..)`: Sorts the input based on the natural/given comparator.
- `peek(..)`: Allows consuming the values held by the stream without changing them.
- `limit(..)`: Truncates the stream elements to the given number.
- `skip(..)`: Discards the first n elements from the stream.

The following code shows the usage of the `peek`, `limit`, and `skip` methods. It calculates the converted-to-Euro expenses for a business trip. The first and the last expenses are non-business related, so they need to be filtered out (as an alternative, the `filter()` method could be used as well). The `peek` method is printing the expenses used in the expense total:

```
jshell> Map<Currency, Double> exchangeToEur = Map.of(Currency.USD, 0.96,
Currency.GBP, 1.56, Currency.EUR, 1.0);
exchangeToEur ==> {USD=0.96, GBP=1.56, EUR=1.0}
jshell> List<Expense> travelExpenses = List.of(new Expense(10,
Currency.EUR, "Souvenir from Munchen"), new Expense(10.5, Currency.EUR,
"Taxi to Munich airport"), new Expense(20, Currency.USD, "Taxi to San
Francisco hotel"), new Expense(30, Currency.USD, "Meal"), new Expense(21.5,
Currency.GBP, "Taxi to San Francisco airport"), new Expense(10,
Currency.GBP, "Souvenir from London"));
travelExpenses ==> [Expense@1b26f7b2, Expense@491cc5c9, Expense@74ad ...
62d5aee, Expense@69b0fd6f]
jshell> travelExpenses.stream().skip(1).limit(4).
...> peek(x -> System.out.println(x.getDescription())).
...> mapToDouble(x -> x.getAmount() * exchangeToEur.get(x.getCurrency())).
...> sum();
Taxi to Munich airport
Taxi to San Francisco hotel
Meal
Taxi to San Francisco airport
$38 ==> 92.03999999999999
```

Besides the `Stream<T>.ofNullable` method presented earlier, Java 9 introduced `dropWhile` and `takeWhile`. Their purpose is to allow developers to better handle infinite streams. In the following code, we will use them to limit the numbers printed between 5 and 10. Removing the upper limit (set by `takeWhile`) will result in an infinite print of increasing numbers (at some point, they will overflow but still continue to increase–use x -> $x + 100\_000$, for example, in the iterate method):

```
jshell> IntStream.iterate(1, x-> x + 1).
...> dropWhile(x -> x < 5).takeWhile(x -> x < 7).
...> forEach(System.out::println);
```

The output is 5 and 6, as expected, since they are bigger than 5 and smaller than 7.

Stream terminal operations

Terminal operations are values or side-effect operations that traverse the pipeline of the intermediate operations and make the appropriate calls. They can process the returned values (`forEach(...)`, `forEachOrdered(...)`) or they can return any of the following:

- An iterator (such as the `iterator()` and `spliterator()` methods)
- A collection (`toArray(...)`, `collect(...)`, by using the Collectors `toList()`, `toSet()`, `toColletion()`, `groupingBy()`, `partitioningBy()`, or `toMap()`)
- A specific element (`findFirst()`, `findAny()`)
- An aggregation (reduction) that could be any of these:
    - **Arithmetic**: `min(...)`, `max(...)`, `count()` or `sum()`, `average()`, and `summaryStatistics()` specific only to `IntStream`, `LongStream`, and `DoubleStream`.
    - **Boolean**: `anyMatch(...)`, `allMatch(...)`, and `noneMatch(...)`.
    - **Custom**: By using the `reduce(...)` or `collect(...)` methods. Some of the available Collectors include `maxBy()`, `minBy()`, `reducing()`, `joining()`, and `counting()`.

Re-implementing OOP design patterns

In this section, we are going to review some of the GOF patterns in light of the new features available in Java 8 and 9.

Singleton

The singleton pattern can be re-implemented by using closure and `Supplier<T>`. The Java hybrid code can make use of the `Supplier<T>` interface, such as in the following code, where the singleton is an enum (according to functional programming, the singleton types are those that have only one value, just like enums). The following example code is similar to the one from `chapter 2`, *Creational Patterns*:

```
jshell> enum Singleton{
...> INSTANCE;
...> public static Supplier<Singleton> getInstance()
...> {
...> return () -> Singleton.INSTANCE;
```

```
...> }
...>
...> public void doSomething(){
...> System.out.println("Something is Done.");
...> }
...> }
| created enum Singleton
jshell> Singleton.getInstance().get().doSomething();
Something is Done.
```

Builder

The Lombock library introduces the builder as part of its features. By just using the @Builder annotation, any class can automatically gain access to a builder method, as the Lombock example code shows at https://projectlombok.org/features/Builder:

```
Person.builder().name("Adam Savage").city("San
Francisco").job("Mythbusters").job("Unchained Reaction").build();
```

Other pre-Java 8 implementations made use of reflection to create a generic builder. The Java 8+ generic builder version can be implemented by leveraging the supplier and the BiConsumer composition, as shown in the following code:

```
jshell> class Person { private String name;
...> public void setName(String name) { this.name = name; }
...> public String getName() { return name; }}
| replaced class Person
| update replaced variable a, reset to null
jshell> Supplier<Person> getPerson = Person::new
getPerson ==> $Lambda$214/2095303566@78b66d36
jshell> Person a = getPerson.get()
a ==> Person@5223e5ee
jshell> a.getName();
$91 ==> null
jshell> BiConsumer<Person, String> changePersonName = (x, y) ->
x.setName(y)
changePersonName ==> $Lambda$215/581318631@6fe7aac8
jshell> changePersonName.accept(a, "Gandalf")
jshell> a.getName();
$94 ==> "Gandalf"
```

Adapter

The best example is the usage of the map function that performs an adaptation from the old interface to the new interface. We are going to reuse the example from Chapter 4, *Structural Patterns*, with a small twist; the map simulates the adapter code:

```
jshell> class PS2Device {};
| created class PS2Device
jshell> class USBDevice {};
| created class USBDevice
jshell> Optional.of(new PS2Device()).stream().map(x -> new
USBDevice()).findFirst().get()
$39 ==> USBDevice@15bb6bea
```

Decorator

The decorator can be implemented by leveraging the function composition. For example, adding logging to an existing function call can be done, as shown earlier, by using the stream peek method and log to the console from the provided peek Consumer<T>.

Our Chapter 4, *Structural Patterns*, decorator example can be rewritten in functional style; notice that the decorator is used to consume the same input as the initial decorated consumer:

```
jshell> Consumer<String> toASCII = x -> System.out.println("Print ASCII: "
+ x);
toASCII ==> $Lambda$159/1690859824@400cff1a
jshell> Function<String, String> toHex = x -> x.chars().boxed().map(y ->
"0x" + Integer.toHexString(y)).collect(Collectors.joining(" "));
toHex ==> $Lambda$158/1860250540@55040f2f
jshell> Consumer<String> decorateToHex = x -> System.out.println("Print
HEX: " + toHex.apply(x))
decorateToHex ==> $Lambda$160/1381965390@75f9eccc
jshell> toASCII.andThen(decorateToHex).accept("text")
Print ASCII: text
Print HEX: 0x74 0x65 0x78 0x74
```

Chain of responsibility

The chain of responsibility can be implemented as a list of handlers (functions), each one performing a specific action. The following example code makes use of closure and a stream of functions that all apply, one after another, on the given text:

```
jshell> String text = "Text";
text ==> "Text"
jshell> Stream.<Function<String, String>>of(String::toLowerCase, x ->
LocalDateTime.now().toString() + " " + x).map(f ->
f.apply(text)).collect(Collectors.toList())
$55 ==> [text, 2017-08-10T08:41:28.243310800 Text]
```

Command

The intent is to convert a method into an object to store it and call it later, be able to track its calls, log, and undo. This is the basic usage of the `Consumer<T>` class.

In the following code, we are going to create a list of commands and execute them one by one:

```
jshell> List<Consumer<String>> tasks = List.of(System.out::println, x ->
System.out.println(LocalDateTime.now().toString() + " " + x))
tasks ==> [$Lambda$192/728258269@6107227e, $Lambda$193/1572098393@7c417213]
jshell> tasks.forEach(x -> x.accept(text))
Text
2017-08-10T08:47:31.673812300 Text
```

Interpreter

The interpreter's grammar can be stored as a map of keywords with the corresponding action stored as a value. In `Chapter 2`, *Creational Patterns*, we used a mathematical expression evaluator that accumulates the result in a stack. This can be implemented by having the expressions stored in a map and accumulate the result by using reduce:

```
jshell> Map<String, IntBinaryOperator> operands = Map.of("+", (x, y) -> x +
y, "-", (x, y) -> x - y)
operands ==> {-=$Lambda$208/1259652483@65466a6a,
+=$Lambda$207/1552978964@4ddced80}
jshell> Arrays.asList("4 5 + 6 -".split(" ")).stream().reduce("0 ", (acc, x)
-> {
...> if (operands.containsKey(x)) {
...> String[] split = acc.split(" ");
```

```
...> System.out.println(acc);
...> acc = split[0] + " " +
operands.get(x).applyAsInt(Integer.valueOf(split[1]),
Integer.valueOf(split[2])) + " ";
...> } else { acc = acc + x + " ";}
...> return acc; }).split(" ")[1]
0 4 5
0 9 6
$76 ==> "3"
```

Iterator

The iterator is partially implemented by the usage of the sequence that the streams provide. Java 8 added the `forEach` method, which receives a consumer as a parameter and behaves just like the previous loop implementation, as can be seen in the following example code:

```
jshell> List.of(1, 4).forEach(System.out::println)
jshell> for(Integer i: List.of(1, 4)) System.out.println(i);
```

The output for each example is 1 and 4, as expected.

Observer

The observer pattern got replaced in Java 8 with lambda expressions. The most obvious example is the `ActionListener` replacement. The old code, using anonymous class listeners, got replaced with a simple function call:

```
JButton button = new Jbutton("Click Here");
button.addActionListener(new ActionListener()
{
  public void actionPerformed(ActionEvent e)
  {
    System.out.println("Handled by the old listener");
  }
});
```

The new code is just one line:

```
button.addActionListener(e -> System.out.println("Handled by lambda"));
```

Strategy

The strategy can be replaced by a function. In the following example code, we apply a 10% discount strategy to all our prices:

```
jshell> Function<Double, Double> tenPercentDiscount = x -> x * 0.9;
tenPercentDiscount ==> $Lambda$217/1990160809@4c9f8c13
jshell> List.<Double>of(5.4, 6.27,
3.29).stream().map(tenPercentDiscount).collect(Collectors.toList())
$98 ==> [4.86, 5.643, 2.9610000000000003]
```

Template method

The template method can be implemented to allow the injection of specific method calls when the template offers the order of calls. In the following examples, we will add specific calls and set their content from outside. They may have specific content already inserted. The code can be simplified by using a single method that received all the runnables:

```
jshell> class TemplateMethod {
...> private Runnable call1 = () -> {};
...> private Runnable call2 = () -> System.out.println("Call2");
...> private Runnable call3 = () -> {};
...> public void setCall1(Runnable call1) { this.call1 = call1;}
...> public void setCall2(Runnable call2) { this.call2 = call2; }
...> public void setCall3(Runnable call3) { this.call3 = call3; }
...> public void run() {
...> call1.run();
...> call2.run();
...> call3.run();
...> }
...> }
| created class TemplateMethod
jshell> TemplateMethod t = new TemplateMethod();
t ==> TemplateMethod@70e8f8e
jshell> t.setCall1(() -> System.out.println("Call1"));
jshell> t.setCall3(() -> System.out.println("Call3"));
jshell> t.run();
Call1
Call2
Call3
```

Functional design patterns

In this section, we are going to learn about the following functional design patterns:

- MapReduce
- Loan pattern
- Tail call optimization
- Memoization
- The execute around method

MapReduce

MapReduce is a technique used for massive parallel programming, developed by Google, which emerged as a functional design pattern because of the ease of expression. In functional programming, it is a form of a monad.

Intent

The intent is to break existing tasks into multiple smaller ones, run them in parallel, and aggregate the result (reduce). It is expected to improve performance for big data.

Examples

We will demonstrate the usage of the MapReduce pattern by parsing and aggregating logs from multiple web services based on a given Sleuth span and calculating the overall duration for each hit endpoint. The logs are taken from `https://cloud.spring.io/spring-cloud-sleuth/spring-cloud-sleuth.html` and split into the corresponding service log file. The following code reads in parallel all the logs, maps, sorts, and filters the relevant log entries, collects and reduces (aggregates) the result. If there is a result, it gets printed to the console. The imported date/time classes are used for the ordering comparison. The `flatMap` code needs to handle `Exception`, as shown in this code:

```
jshell> import java.time.*
jshell> import java.time.format.*
jshell> DateTimeFormatter dtf = DateTimeFormatter.ofPattern("yyyy-MM-dd
HH:mm:ss.SSS")
dtf ==> Value(YearOfEra,4,19,EXCEEDS_PAD)'-'Value(MonthOf ...
Fraction(NanoOfSecond,3,3)
jshell> try (Stream<Path> files = Files.find(Paths.get("d:/"), 1, (path,
```

```
attr) -> String.valueOf(path).endsWith(".log"))) {
...> files.parallel().
...> flatMap(x -> { try { return Files.lines(x); } catch (IOException e) {}
return null;}).
...> filter(x -> x.contains("2485ec27856c56f4")).
...> map(x -> x.substring(0, 23) + " " + x.split(":")[3]).
...> sorted((x, y) -> LocalDateTime.parse(x.substring(0, 23),
dtf).compareTo(LocalDateTime.parse(y.substring(0, 23), dtf))).
...> collect(Collectors.toList()).stream().sequential().
...> reduce((acc, x) -> {
...> if (acc.length() > 0) {
...> Long duration =
Long.valueOf(Duration.between(LocalDateTime.parse(acc.substring(0, 23),
dtf), LocalDateTime.parse(x.substring(0, 23), dtf)).t oMillis());
...> acc += "n After " + duration.toString() + "ms " + x.substring(24);
...> } else {
...> acc = x;
...> }
...> return acc;}).ifPresent(System.out::println);
...> }
2016-02-26 11:15:47.561 Hello from service1. Calling service2
After 149ms Hello from service2. Calling service3 and then service4
After 334ms Hello from service3
After 363ms Got response from service3 [Hello from service3]
After 573ms Hello from service4
After 595ms Got response from service4 [Hello from service4]
After 621ms Got response from service2 [Hello from service2, response from
service3 [Hello from service3] and from service4 [Hello from service4]]
```

Loan pattern

The Loan pattern ensures that a resource is deterministically disposed of once it goes out of scope. A resource could be one of a database connection, file, socket, or any object that handles a native resource (memory, system handles, connections of any type). This is similar in intent to the Dispose Pattern described on MSDN.

Intent

The intent is to free the user from the burden of releasing unused resources once they are used. The user may forget to call the release method of the resource, resulting in a leak.

Examples

One of the most-used templates when working with database transaction is getting a transaction, making the appropriate calls, and making sure to commit or rollback on exception and close the transaction. This can be implemented as a loan pattern, where the moving part is the calls within the transaction. The following code shows how this can be achieved:

```
jshell> class Connection {
...> public void commit() {};
public void rollback() {};
public void close() {};
public void setAutoCommit(boolean autoCommit) {};
...> public static void runWithinTransaction(Consumer<Connection> c) {
...> Connection t = null;
...> try { t = new Connection(); t.setAutoCommit(false);
...> c.accept(t);
...> t.commit();
...> } catch(Exception e) { t.rollback(); } finally { t.close(); } } }
| created class Connection
jshell> Connection.runWithinTransaction(x -> System.out.println("Execute
statement...") );
Execute statement...
```

Tail call optimization

Tail call optimization (TCO) is a technique used by some compilers to call a function without using stack space. Scala makes use of it by annotating the recursive code with the `@tailrec` annotation. This basically tells the compiler to use a special loop, called trampoline, that repeatedly runs functions. A function call could be in one of the states—done or more to call. On done, it returns the result (head), and on more, it returns the current loop without the head (tail). This pattern is already made available to us by the cyclops-react library.

Intent

The intent is to enable recursive calls without blowing up the stack. It is intended to be used only for a high number of recursive calls, for a few calls, it may decrease performance.

Examples

John McClean, the maintainer of cyclops-react, demos the usage of TCO that calculates numbers in the Fibonacci sequence at `https://gist.github.com/johnmcclean/fb1735b49e6206396bd5792ca11ba7b2`. The code is clean and simple to understand; it basically accumulates Fibonacci numbers starting from the initial states—a and b, $f(0) = 0$, $f(1) = 1$—and applying the $f(n) = f(n-1) + f(n-2)$ functions:

```java
importstatic cyclops.control.Trampoline.done;
importstatic cyclops.control.Trampoline.more;
import cyclops.control.Trampoline;
publicclass Main
{
  publicvoid fib()
  {
    for(int i=0;i<100_000;i++)
    System.out.println(fibonacci(i, 0l, 1l).get());
  }
  public Trampoline<Long> fibonacci(Integer count, Long a, Long b)
  {
    return count==0 ? done(a) : more(()->fibonacci (count - 1,
    b, a + b));
  }
  publicstaticvoid main(String[] args)
  {
    new Main().fib();
  }
}
```

Memoization

Calling the preceding Fibonacci implementation multiple times will result in a waste of CPU cycles, since some steps are the same and we are guaranteed that, for the same input, we'll always get the same output (pure function). To speed up the call, we can cache the output, and for the given input, just return the cached result, instead of actually calculating it.

Intent

The intent is to cache the result of a function for a given input and use it to speed up further calls to the same function given the same input. It should be used only for pure functions, since they provide referential transparency.

Examples

In the following example, we are going to reuse the Fibonacci code and add a Guava cache. The cache will hold the returned values of Fibonacci while the key is the input number. The cache is configured to limit the memory footprint both in size and time:

```java
importstatic cyclops.control.Trampoline.done;
importstatic cyclops.control.Trampoline.more;
import java.math.BigInteger;
import java.util.Arrays;
import java.util.List;
import java.util.concurrent.TimeUnit;
import com.google.common.cache.Cache;
import com.google.common.cache.CacheBuilder;
import cyclops.async.LazyReact;
import cyclops.control.Trampoline;
publicclass Main
{
  public BigInteger fib(BigInteger n)
  {
    return fibonacci(n, BigInteger.ZERO, BigInteger.ONE).get();
  }
  public Trampoline<BigInteger> fibonacci(BigInteger count,
  BigInteger a, BigInteger b)
  {
    return count.equals(BigInteger.ZERO) ? done(a) :
    more(()->fibonacci (count.subtract(BigInteger.ONE), b,
    a.add(b)));
  }
  publicvoid memoization(List<Integer> array)
  {
    Cache<BigInteger, BigInteger> cache = CacheBuilder.newBuilder()
    .maximumSize(1_000_000)
    .expireAfterWrite(10, TimeUnit.MINUTES)
    .build();
    LazyReact react = new LazyReact().autoMemoizeOn((key,fn)->
    cache.get((BigInteger)key,()-> (BigInteger)fn.
    apply((BigInteger)key)));
    Listresult = react.from(array)
    .map(i->fibonacci(BigInteger.valueOf(i), BigInteger.ZERO,
    BigInteger.ONE))
    .toList();
  }
  publicstaticvoid main(String[] args)
  {
    Main main = new Main();
    List<Integer> array = Arrays.asList(500_000, 499_999);
```

```
        long start = System.currentTimeMillis();
        array.stream().map(BigInteger::valueOf).forEach(x -> main.fib(x));
        System.out.println("Regular version took " +
        (System.currentTimeMillis() - start) + " ms");
        start = System.currentTimeMillis();
        main.memoization(array);
        System.out.println("Memoized version took " +
        (System.currentTimeMillis() - start) + " ms");
    }
}
```

The output is as follows:

```
Regular version took 19022 ms
Memoized version took 394 ms
```

The execute around method

The preceding code seems to repeat itself when measuring the performance of each version of the code. This can be fixed with the execute around method pattern, by wrapping the executed business code inside a lambda expression. A good example of this pattern is the before and after unit test setup/teardown functions. This is similar to the template method and the loan pattern described before.

Intent

The intent is to free the user for some certain actions that are to be executed before and after a specific business method.

Examples

The code mentioned in the previous example contains duplicated code (code smell). We'll apply the execute around pattern to simplify the code and make it easier to read. A possible refactoring can make use of lambda, as we can see:

```
publicstaticvoid measurePerformance(Runnable runnable)
{
  long start = System.currentTimeMillis();
  runnable.run();
  System.out.println("It took " + (System.currentTimeMillis() -
  start) + " ms");
}
```

```
publicstaticvoid main(String[] args)
{
  Main main = new Main();
  List<Integer> array = Arrays.asList(500_000, 499_999);
  measurePerformance(() -> array.stream().map(BigInteger::valueOf)
  .forEach(x -> main.fib(x)));
  measurePerformance(() -> main.memoization(array));
}
```

Summary

In this chapter, we learned what functional programming means, the features provided by the latest Java versions, and how they've changed some of the existing GOF patterns. We also made use of some functional programming design patterns.

In the next chapter, we'll dive into the reactive world and learn how to create responsive applications with RxJava.

6
Let's Get Reactive

This chapter will describe the reactive programming paradigm and why it works very well for languages with functional elements. The reader will be familiarized with the concepts behind reactive programming. We will present the elements used from both the observer pattern and the iterator pattern in creating a reactive application. The examples will make use of the Reactive Framework and a Java implementation called **RxJava** (version 2.0).

We will cover the following topics:

- What is reactive programming?
- Introduction to RxJava
- Installing RxJava
- Observable, Flowable, Observers, and Subscriptions
- Creating Observables
- Transforming Observables
- Filtering Observables
- Combining Observables
- Error-handling
- Schedulers
- Subjects
- Example project

What is reactive programming?

According to *The Reactive Manifesto* (http://www.reactivemanifesto.org/), reactive systems have the following attributes:

- **Responsive**: The system responds in a timely manner in a consistent and predictable way.

- **Resilient**: The system is resilient to faults and can quickly recover from them.
- **Elastic**: The system maintains its responsiveness under varying workloads, by increasing or decreasing the resources allocated. This is done by dynamically finding and fixing bottlenecks. This is not to be confused with scalability. An elastic system needs to be scalable up and down according to need–see `http://www.reactivemanifesto.org/glossary#Elasticity`.
- **Message-driven**: They rely on asynchronous message-passing that ensures loose coupling, isolation, location transparency, and fault tolerance.

The need is real. Nowadays, a non-responsive system is considered buggy and will be avoided by customers. A non-responsive website will have a low rank in search engines, according to `https://developers.google.com/search/mobile-sites/mobile-seo/`:

"responsive design is Google's recommended design pattern"

A reactive system is an architectural style of composing a complex system by using elements, some built with reactive programming techniques.

Reactive programming is a paradigm that relies on asynchronous data streams. It is an event-driven subset of asynchronous programming. In contrast, reactive systems are message-driven, that means that the recipient is known upfront, while for events the recipients can be any observer.

Reactive programming is more than event-based programming because it makes use of data flows–it emphasizes the flow of data rather than the flow of control. Earlier, events such as mouse or keyboard events, or backend events, such as new socket connection on the server, would have been handled in a thread event loop (thread-of-execution). Now everything can be used to create a data stream; imagine that the JSON REST response from one of the backend endpoints becomes a data stream and it can be awaited, filtered, or merged with some other response from a different endpoint. This approach provides a lot of flexibility by removing the need for the developer to explicitly create all the boilerplate code that handles the asynchronous calls in multi-core and multi-CPU environments.

One of the best and most overused examples of reactive programming examples is the spreadsheet example. Defining a stream (flow) is similar to declaring that the value of Excel's C1 cell equals the content of the B1 cell plus the A1 cell. Whenever the A1 or B1 cells are updated, the change is observed and reacted upon, and the side-effect is that the C1 value gets updated. Now imagine that C2 to Cn cells are equal to the content of A2 to An plus B2 to Bn; the same rule applies to all.

Reactive programming is applied using some of the following programming abstractions, some taken from the functional programming world:

- **Futures/promises**: These provide the means to act on values that are to be provided somewhere in the near future.
- **Stream**: This provides the data pipeline, just like a train track that provides the infrastructure for the train to run on.
- **Dataflow variables**: These are results of the functions applied to the stream function's input variables, just like the spreadsheet cell that is set by applying the plus mathematical function on the two given input parameters.
- **Throttling**: This mechanism is used in real-time processing environments, including hardware such as **digital signal processors** (**DSP**), to regulate the speed of input-processing by dropping elements in order to catch up with the input speed; it is used as a back-pressure strategy.
- **Push mechanism**: This is similar to the Hollywood principle since it reverses the calling direction. Once the data is available, the relevant observers in the flow are called to do the processing of the data; in contrast, the pull mechanism grabs the information in a synchronous way.

There are numerous Java libraries and frameworks that allow programmers to write reactive code, such as Reactor, Ratpack, RxJava, Spring Framework 5, and Vert.x. With the addition of the JDK 9 Flow API, reactive programming is made available for developers without the need to install additional APIs.

Introduction to RxJava

RxJava is an implementation of reactive extension (a library for composing asynchronous and event-based programs by using observable sequences) ported from the Microsoft .NET world. In 2012, Netflix realized that they needed a paradigm shift since their architecture could not cope with their huge customer base, so they decided to go reactive by bringing the power of the reactive extension to the JVM world; this is how RxJava was born. There are other JVM implementations besides RxJava, such as RxAndroid, RxJavaFX, RxKotlin, and RxScale. This approach gave them the desired boost, and by making it publicly available, it also offered us the opportunity to use it.

RxJava JAR is licensed under the Apache Software License, version 2.0, and available in the central maven repository.

There are a couple of external libraries that make use of RxJava:

- `hystrix`: A latency and fault-tolerant library designed to isolate points of access to remote systems
- `rxjava-http-tail`: An HTTP log-following library usable in the same way as `tail -f`
- `rxjava-jdbc`: This uses RxJava with JDBC connections to the `ResultSets` stream

Installing the RxJava framework

In this section, we'll cover RxJava installation from Maven (Gradle, SBT, Ivy, Grape, Leiningen, or Buildr steps are similar) and usage from Java 9's REPL Jshell.

Maven installation

Installing the RxJava framework is easy. The JAR file and the dependent project reactive stream are available under maven at `http://central.maven.org/maven2/io/reactivex/rxjava2/rxjava/2.1.3/rxjava-2.1.3.jar`.

In order to use it, include this maven dependency in your `pom.xml` file:

```
<project xmlns="http://maven.apache.org/POM/4.0.0"
xmlns:xsi="http://www.w3.org/2001/XMLSchema-instance"
xsi:schemaLocation="http://maven.apache.org/POM/4.0.0
http://maven.apache.org/xsd/maven-4.0.0.xsd">
  <modelVersion>4.0.0</modelVersion>
  <groupId>com.packt.java9</groupId>
  <artifactId>chapter6_client</artifactId>
  <version>0.0.1-SNAPSHOT</version>
  <properties>
    <maven.compiler.source>1.8</maven.compiler.source>
    <maven.compiler.target>1.8</maven.compiler.target>
  </properties>
  <dependencies>
    <!-- https://mvnrepository.com/artifact/io.reactivex.
    rxjava2/rxjava -->
    <dependency>
      <groupId>io.reactivex.rxjava2</groupId>
      <artifactId>rxjava</artifactId>
      <version>2.1.3</version>
    </dependency>
```

```
<!-- https://mvnrepository.com/artifact/org.
reactivestreams/reactive-streams -->
<dependency>
  <groupId>org.reactivestreams</groupId>
  <artifactId>reactive-streams</artifactId>
  <version>1.0.1</version>
</dependency>
</dependencies>
</project>
```

Installing in Gradle, SBT, Ivy, Grape, Leiningen, or Buildr is similar; check out `https://mvnrepository.com/artifact/io.reactivex.rxjava2/rxjava/2.1.3` for more information on what needs to be added to the `configuration` file.

JShell installation

We will discuss JShell in detail in `Chapter 9`, *Best Practices in Java*, for now, let's take a look at it from the RxJava perspective. Installing the RxJava framework in JShell is done by setting the classpath to both RxJava and reactive streams JAR files. Notice the use of the colon on Linux and the semi-colon on Windows as the file path separator:

```
"c:Program FilesJavajdk-9binjshell" --class-path
D:KitsrxjavarxJava-2.1.3.jar;D:Kitsrxjavareactive-streams-1.0.1.jar
```

The following error will be displayed on your screen:

```
jshell> Observable.just("Hello World!")
|  Error:
|  cannot find symbol
|    symbol:   method just(java.lang.String)
|  Observable.just("Hello World!")
|  ^--------------^
```

The preceding error happened because we forgot to import the relevant Java class.

Following code handles this error:

```
jshell> import io.reactivex.Observable

jshell> Observable.just("Hello World!")
$2 ==> io.reactivex.internal.operators.observable.ObservableJust@74ad1f1f
```

Now we've managed to create our first observable. In the following sections, we will learn what it does and how to use it.

Observables, Flowables, Observers, and Subscriptions

In ReactiveX, an observer subscribes to an Observable. When the Observable emits data, the observer reacts by consuming or transforming the data. This pattern facilitates concurrent operations because it does not need to block while waiting for the Observable to emit objects. Instead, it creates a sentry in the form of an observer that stands ready to react appropriately whenever new data in the form of an Observable is available. This model is referred to as the reactor pattern. The following diagram, taken from `http://reactivex.io/assets/operators/legend.png`, explains the flow of Observables:

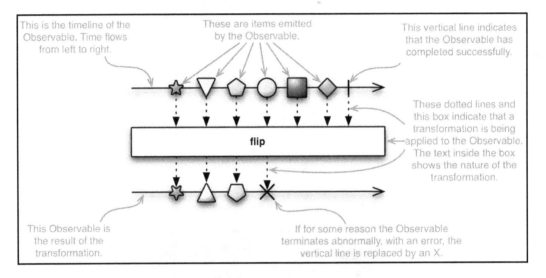

Reactive's Observable is similar to the imperative Iterable. It addresses the same problem but the strategy is different. The Observable works by pushing changes, once available, asynchronously, while the Iterable pulls the changes mechanism in a synchronous way. The way to deal with the errors is different too; one uses an error callback while the other uses side-effects, such as throwing exceptions. The following table shows the differences:

Event	Iterable	Observable
Get Data	`T next()`	`onNext(T)`
Error	`throw new Exception`	`onError(Exception)`
Done	`Return`	`onCompleted()`

Connecting an observer to an Observable is done by using the subscribe (`onNextAction`, `onErrorAction`, `onCompletedAction`) method. The observer implements some subset of the following methods (only the `onNext` is mandatory):

- `onNext`: This is called whenever the Observable emits an item and the method takes the item emitted by the Observable as a parameter
- `onError`: This is called to indicate that it has failed to generate the expected data or has encountered some other error and takes the exception/error as its parameter
- `onCompleted`: This is called when there is no more data to emit

From design perspectives, the Reactive Observable enhances the Gang of Four's Observer pattern by adding the capability to signal on completion and on error by using the `onError` and `onCompleted` callbacks.

There are two types of Reactive Observables:

- **Hot**: Starts emitting as soon as possible even if no subscribers are attached.
- **Cold**: Waits for at least one subscriber to attach before starting to emit data, therefore at least one subscriber may see the sequence from the beginning. They are called "Connectable" observables and RxJava has operators that enable creating such Observables.

RxJava 2.0 introduced a new type of Observable, called Flowable. The new `io.reactivex.Flowable` is a back-pressure-enabled base reactive class, while the Observable is not anymore. Back-pressure is a set of strategies used to cope with situations when the observables emit more data that the subscribers can handle.

The RxJava Observable should be used for small sets of data (no more than 1,000 elements at its longest) in order to prevent `OutOfMemoryError` or for GUI events, such as mouse moves or touch events at a small frequency (1,000 Hz or less).

Flowables are to be used when dealing with more than 10,000 elements, reading (parsing) files from disk, which works well with back-pressure, reading from a database through JDBC, or doing blocking and/or pull-based data reads.

Creating Observables

The following operators are used to create Observables from scratch, out of existing objects, arrays of other data structure, or by a sequence or timer.

The create operator

Creating Observables from scratch can be done by calling one of the following `io.reactivex.Observable` methods (operators):

- Create
- Generate
- UnsafeCreate

The following example shows how to construct an Observable from scratch. Call `onNext()` until the observer is not disposed, `onComplete()` and `onError()` programmatically in order to get a 1 to 4 range of numbers:

```
jshell> io.reactivex.Observable.create(observer -> {
   ...>         try {
   ...>             if (!observer.isDisposed()) {
   ...>                 for (int i = 1; i < 5; i++) {
   ...>                     observer.onNext(i);
   ...>                 }
   ...>                 observer.onComplete();
   ...>             }
   ...>         } catch (Exception e) {
   ...>             observer.onError(e);
   ...>         }
   ...>     }).subscribe(System.out::println, System.err::println, () -> System.out.println("Sequence complete."));
1
2
3
4
Sequence complete.
$1 ==> DISPOSED

jshell>
```

As we can see in the preceding screenshot, the output is as expected, range from 1 to 4, and the sequence gets disposed of after usage.

The defer operator

Creating a new Observable for each observer once the observer connects can be done by calling the `defer` method. The following code shows the usage of `defer` for the case when we supply a number:

```
jshell> io.reactivex.Observable<Integer> a = io.reactivex.Observable.defer(() -> io.reactivex.Observable.just(123))
a ==> io.reactivex.internal.operators.observable.ObservableDefer@fe18270

jshell> a.subscribe(System.out::println);
123
$5 ==> DISPOSED
```

The console print-line method outputs 123, which is the Observable-wrapped integer.

The empty operator

Creating empty, a never sending item, can be done by calling the `empty()` or `never()` `io.reactivex.Observable` methods.

The from operator

Converting from an arrays, futures, or other objects and data structures can be done by calling one of the following methods:

- `fromArray`: Converts an array to an Observable
- `fromCallable`: Converts a callable that supplies a value to an Observable
- `fromFuture`: Converts a future provided value to an Observable
- `fromIterable`: Converts an iterable to an Observable
- `fromPublisher`: Converts a reactive publisher stream to an Observable
- `just`: Converts a given object to an Observable

The following example creates an Observable out of a list of letters (`abc`):

```
jshell> io.reactivex.Observable<String> abc = io.reactivex.Observable.fromArray("a", "b", "c");
abc ==> io.reactivex.internal.operators.observable.ObservableFromArray@3b94d659

jshell> abc.subscribe(System.out::println);
a
b
c
$7 ==> DISPOSED
```

The entire array of a, b, and c is consumed and printed to the console by the `System.out.println` method.

The interval operator

Creating an Observable that emits a sequence of integers spaced by a particular time interval can be done by using the `interval` method. The following example never stops; it continuously prints the tick number every one second:

```
jshell> io.reactivex.Observable.interval(1, TimeUnit.SECONDS).
   ...>     map(tick -> tick.longValue()).subscribe(System.out::println);
$1 ==> io.reactivex.internal.operators.observable.ObservableMap$MapObserver@17776a8

jshell> 0

jshell> 1
2

jshell>

jshell> 3
4
5
6
7
```

Trying to stop the timer won't help (not even *Ctrl* + *C*, just close the window), it will continue to print the incremented number to the console every one second, just as instructed.

The timer operator

Emitting a single item after a given delay can be done by using the timer method.

The range operator

Creating ranges of sequential numbers can be achieved by using the following methods:

- `intervalRange`: Signals a range of long values, the first after some initial delay and the following periodically
- `range`: Emits a sequence of integers within a specified range

The repeat operator

In order to repeat a particular item or a specific sequence use:

- `repeat`: Repeats the sequence of items emitted by the given Observable source a number of times or forever (depending on the input)
- `repeatUntil`: Repeats the sequence of items emitted by the Observable source until the provided stop function returns true
- `repeatWhen`: Emits the same values as the initial Observable with the exception of `onComplete`

The following code repeats the given value of a until the condition is satisfied:

```
jshell> Integer x = 1
x ==> 1

jshell> io.reactivex.Observable.just('a').
   ...>    repeatUntil(() -> x++ > 2).subscribe(System.out::println);
a
a
a
$9 ==> DISPOSED
```

It repeats a to the console three times until x has value 3 which is bigger than 2. As an exercise, replace x++ with ++x and check the console.

Transforming Observables

These are the operators that transform items emitted by an Observable.

The subscribe operator

These are the methods used by a subscriber to consume the emissions and notifications from an Observable, such as `onNext`, `onError`, and `onCompleted`. The Observable methods used for subscribing are:

- `blockingForEach`: Consumes each item emitted by this Observable and blocks until the Observable completes.
- `blockingSubscribe`: Subscribes to the Observable and consumes events on the current thread.

- `forEachWhile`: Subscribes to the Observable and receives notifications for each element until the `onNext` Predicate returns false.
- `forEach`: Subscribes to the Observable and receives notifications for each element.
- `subscribe`: Subscribes the given observer to this Observable. The observer can be given as callbacks, observer implementations, or subtypes of the abstract `io.reactivex.subscribers.DefaultSubscriber<T>` class.

The buffer operator

The `buffer` method is used to create bundles of a given size, then pack them as lists. The following code shows how, out of 10 numbers, we created two bundles, one with six and the other with the remaining four items:

```
jshell> io.reactivex.Observable.range(0, 10).
   ...>      buffer(6).subscribe(System.out::println);
[0, 1, 2, 3, 4, 5]
[6, 7, 8, 9]
$13 ==> DISPOSED
```

The flatMap operator

Transforming the given Observables into a single Observable either by the arrival order (`flatMap`), keeping the last emitted (`switchMap`), or by preserving the original order (`concatMap`) can be done by using one of the following operators: `concatMap`, `concatMapDelayError`, `concatMapEager`, `concatMapEagerDelayError`, `concatMapIterable`, `flatMap`, `flatMapIterable`, `switchMap`, or `switchMapDelayError`. The following example shows how by randomly choosing the order of observables, the content of the output changes. (`flatMap`, `concatMap`, and `switchMap`):

```
jshell> import io.reactivex.schedulers.TestScheduler

jshell> TestScheduler scheduler = new TestScheduler();
scheduler ==> io.reactivex.schedulers.TestScheduler@5f71c76a

jshell> io.reactivex.Observable<String> abc = io.reactivex.Observable.fromArray("a", "b", "c");
abc ==> io.reactivex.internal.operators.observable.ObservableFromArray@1d7acb34

jshell> abc.concatMap( x -> io.reactivex.Observable.just(x + "c").
   ...>      delay(new Random().nextInt(5), TimeUnit.SECONDS, scheduler)).
   ...>      toList().subscribe(System.out::println,System.out::println);
$20 ==> io.reactivex.internal.operators.observable.ObservableToListSingle$ToListObserver@176d53b2

jshell> scheduler.advanceTimeBy(30, TimeUnit.SECONDS);
[ac, bc, cc]
```

The concatMap implementation is appending the c string to each of the given a, b, and c strings, therefore, the output is ac, bc, and cc.

The flatMap implementation is appending the f string to each of the given a, b, and c strings, as follows:

```
jshell> abc.flatMap( x -> io.reactivex.Observable.just(x + "f").
   ...>      delay(new Random().nextInt(5), TimeUnit.SECONDS, scheduler)).
   ...>      toList().subscribe(System.out::println,System.out::println);
$38 ==> io.reactivex.internal.operators.observable.ObservableToListSingle$ToListObserver@59d016c9

jshell> scheduler.advanceTimeBy(30, TimeUnit.SECONDS);
[cf, bf, af]

jshell> abc.flatMap( x -> io.reactivex.Observable.just(x + "f").
   ...>      delay(new Random().nextInt(5), TimeUnit.SECONDS, scheduler)).
   ...>      toList().subscribe(System.out::println,System.out::println);
$40 ==> io.reactivex.internal.operators.observable.ObservableToListSingle$ToListObserver@7c0c77c7

jshell> scheduler.advanceTimeBy(30, TimeUnit.SECONDS);
[af, cf, bf]

jshell> abc.flatMap( x -> io.reactivex.Observable.just(x + "f").
   ...>      delay(new Random().nextInt(5), TimeUnit.SECONDS, scheduler)).
   ...>      toList().subscribe(System.out::println,System.out::println);
$42 ==> io.reactivex.internal.operators.observable.ObservableToListSingle$ToListObserver@65466a6a

jshell> scheduler.advanceTimeBy(30, TimeUnit.SECONDS);
[af, bf, cf]
```

Because of the random delay, the order is different from the expected af, bf, and cf; running it a couple of times will output the expected order.

Following snippet shows a different output.

```
jshell> abc.switchMap( x -> io.reactivex.Observable.just(x + "s").
   ...>     delay(new Random().nextInt(5), TimeUnit.SECONDS, scheduler)).
   ...>     toList().subscribe(System.out::println,System.out::println);
$24 ==> io.reactivex.internal.operators.observable.ObservableToListSingle$ToListObserver@d4342c2

jshell> scheduler.advanceTimeBy(30, TimeUnit.SECONDS);
[cs]
```

The `switchMap` implementation is appending the `s` string to the last element from the given `a`, `b`, and `c` strings list.

Notice the usage of `advanceTimeBy`. Without this call, nothing gets printed since the emissions are delayed.

The groupBy operator

`groupBy` is used to divide an Observable into a set of Observables that each emit a different group of items. The following code groups strings by the starting letter and then prints the keys and the group data for the specific key. Notice that the groups are Observables that can be used to construct other dataflows.

The following output shows the groups by the first letter as a group and also the group key, which is the first letter:

```
jshell> import io.reactivex.observables.*

jshell> io.reactivex.Observable<String> list = io.reactivex.Observable.
   ...> fromArray("aaa", "baa", "ac", "ccc", "ccs");
list ==> io.reactivex.internal.operators.observable.ObservableFromArray@6a400542

jshell> list.groupBy(y -> y.substring(0, 1)).
   ...>   subscribe(x ->
   ...>   {
   ...>     GroupedObservable<String, String> g = (GroupedObservable<String, String>)x;
   ...>     System.out.println(" --- " + g.getKey() + " --- ");
   ...>     g.subscribe(System.out::println);
   ...>   });
 --- a ---
aaa
 --- b ---
baa
ac
 --- c ---
ccc
ccs
$69 ==> DISPOSED
```

The map operator

Applying a function for each item that transforms the Observable can be achieved with:

- `cast`: Casts the result to a given type
- `map`: Applies a specified function to each item emitted

The scan operator

Transformations that make use of accumulation can be done using the `scan` method. The following code makes use of it by emitting the current sum of elements:

```
jshell> io.reactivex.Observable.range(1, 5).
   ...> scan((x, sum) -> x + sum).subscribe(System.out::println);
1
3
6
10
15
$70 ==> DISPOSED
```

The window operator

The `window` method is used to periodically subdivide items from an Observable into Observable windows and burst-emit those windows. The following code shows that using a window of one element does nothing, while using three elements at a time outputs their sum:

```
jshell> io.reactivex.Observable.range(1, 5).
   ...>    window(1).flatMap(x -> x.scan((y, s)  -> y + s)).
   ...>    subscribe(System.out::println);
1
2
3
4
5
$71 ==> DISPOSED
```

Filtering Observables

These are the operators that selectively emit items from a given Observable based on a given condition/constraint.

The debounce operator

Emitting only after a specific timespan has passed can be done using these methods:

- debounce: Mirrors the initial Observable, except that it drops items emitted by the source that are followed by another item within a period of time
- throttleWithTimeout: Emits only those items that are not followed by another emitted item within a specified time window

In the following example, we'll drop items that are fired before our debounce timespan of 100 ms has passed; in our case it is just the last value managed. Again, by using the test scheduler, we advance the time:

```
jshell> TestScheduler scheduler = new TestScheduler();
scheduler ==> io.reactivex.schedulers.TestScheduler@39529185

jshell> io.reactivex.Observable.range(1, 5).
   ...>   flatMap(x -> io.reactivex.Observable.just(x).
   ...>   delay(new Random().nextInt(200), TimeUnit.MILLISECONDS, scheduler)).
   ...>   debounce(100, TimeUnit.MILLISECONDS).
   ...>   subscribe(System.out::println);
$73 ==> io.reactivex.observers.SerializedObserver@515aebb0

jshell> scheduler.advanceTimeBy(1, TimeUnit.MINUTES);
2

jshell>
```

The distinct operator

This removes distinct items emitted by an Observable using the following methods:

- distinct: Emits only distinct elements
- distinctUntilChanged: Emits only elements that are distinct from their immediate predecessors

In the following code, we will see how to use the `distinct` method in order to remove duplicates from a given sequence:

```
jshell> io.reactivex.Observable<String> list =
   ...> io.reactivex.Observable.fromArray("aaa", "baa", "ac", "ccc", "aaa");
list ==> io.reactivex.internal.operators.observable.ObservableFromArray@36bc55de

jshell> list.distinct().subscribe(System.out::println);
aaa
baa
ac
ccc
$76 ==> DISPOSED
```

We can see that the duplicate `aaa` string has been removed from the output.

The elementAt operator

In order to get an element by index, use the `elementAt` method. The following code prints the third element in the list:

```
jshell> io.reactivex.Observable<String> list =
   ...> io.reactivex.Observable.fromArray("aaa", "baa", "ac", "ccc", "aaa");
list ==> io.reactivex.internal.operators.observable.ObservableFromArray@158d2680

jshell> list.elementAt(3).subscribe(System.out::println);
ccc
$78 ==> DISPOSED
```

The filter operator

Using on the following method allows emitting only those items from an Observable that pass a test (predicate/type test):

- `filter`: Emit only elements that satisfy a specified predicate
- `ofType`: Emit only those elements of the specified type

The following code shows the usage of the `filter` method, used to filter out elements not starting with the letter `a`:

```
jshell> io.reactivex.Observable<String> list =
   ...> io.reactivex.Observable.fromArray("aaa", "baa", "ac", "ccc", "aaa");
list ==> io.reactivex.internal.operators.observable.ObservableFromArray@4c402120

jshell> list.filter(x -> x.startsWith("a")).
   ...>   subscribe(System.out::println);
aaa
ac
aaa
$80 ==> DISPOSED
```

The first/last operator

These methods are used to return the first and last occurrence of an item, based on the given condition. There are blocking versions available too. The available `io.reactivex.Observable methods` are:

- `blockingFirst`: Returns the first item emitted by the Observable
- `blockingSingle`: Returns the first `Single` item emitted by the Observable
- `first`: Returns the first item emitted by the Observable
- `firstElement`: Returns a `Maybe` that emits only the very first item
- `single`: Returns a `Single` that emits only the very first item
- `singleElement`: Returns a `Maybe` that emits only the very first Single
- `blockingLast`: Returns the last item emitted by the Observable
- `last`: Returns the last item emitted by the Observable
- `lastElement`: Returns a `Maybe` that emits only the very last Single

The sample operator

Use this operator in order to emit a specific item (specified by the sampling time period or the throttle duration). `io.reactivex.Observable` provides the following methods:

- `sample`: Emits the most recently emitted item (if any) emitted within a given time period

- `throttleFirst`: Emits only the first item emitted during the given sequential time window
- `throttleLast`: Emits only the last item emitted during the given sequential time window

The skip operator

Removes the first and last *n* elements from the output Observable. The following code shows how to skip the first three elements from a given input:

```
jshell> io.reactivex.Observable.range(1, 5).
   ...>    skip(3).subscribe(System.out::println);
4
5
$81 ==> DISPOSED
```

Calling the `skipLast` method would output 1 and 2 only.

The take operator

This emits only the first and last *n* elements from a given Observable. The following example shows how to take only the first three elements from an Observable numeric range:

```
jshell> io.reactivex.Observable.range(1, 5).
   ...>    take(3).subscribe(System.out::println)
1
2
3
$82 ==> DISPOSED
```

Using the `takeLast` method with the same parameter will output 3, 4, and 5.

Combining Observables

These are operators used to combine multiple Observables.

The combine operator

Combining the latest-emitted value from two or more Observables is done by calling one of these methods:

- `combineLatest`: Emits an item that aggregates the latest values of each of the sources
- `withLatestFrom`: Merges the given Observable into the current instance

The following example (runs forever) shows the result of combining two interval observables with different timespans–the first emits every 6 ms, the other every 10 ms:

```
jshell> io.reactivex.Observable a =
   ...> io.reactivex.Observable.interval(6, TimeUnit.MILLISECONDS);
a ==> io.reactivex.internal.operators.observable.ObservableInterval@682b2fa

jshell> io.reactivex.Observable b =
   ...> io.reactivex.Observable.interval(10, TimeUnit.MILLISECONDS);
b ==> io.reactivex.internal.operators.observable.ObservableInterval@7dcf94f8

jshell> io.reactivex.Observable.combineLatest(a, b,
   ...>     (x, y) -> x.toString() + " - " + y.toString()).
   ...>     blockingForEach(System.out::println);
1 - 0
1 - 1
1 - 2
2 - 2
3 - 2
4 - 2
```

The execution of the preceding code needs to be stopped by pressing *Ctrl* + *C* since it creates an infinite list. The output is as expected, it contains the combined values of both sequences based on the creating timestamp.

The join operator

Combining two Observables based on a given window can be done by calling one of the following methods:

- `join`: Joins the items emitted by two Observables based on overlapping durations using an aggregation function
- `groupJoin`: Joins the items emitted by two Observables into groups based on overlapping durations using an aggregation function

The following example uses join to combine two Observables, one firing every 100 ms, the other every 160 ms and taking values from the first every 55 ms and from the second every 85 ms:

```
jshell> io.reactivex.Observable<String> a =
   ...>  io.reactivex.Observable.interval(100, TimeUnit.MILLISECONDS).
   ...>  map(x -> "A"  + x);
a ==> io.reactivex.internal.operators.observable.ObservableMap@5a45133e

jshell> io.reactivex.Observable<String> b =
   ...>  io.reactivex.Observable.interval(160, TimeUnit.MILLISECONDS).
   ...>  map(x -> "B"  + x);
b ==> io.reactivex.internal.operators.observable.ObservableMap@4f80542f

jshell> a.join(b,
   ...>   c -> io.reactivex.Observable.timer(55, TimeUnit.MILLISECONDS),
   ...>   d -> io.reactivex.Observable.timer(85, TimeUnit.MILLISECONDS),
   ...>   (x, y) -> x + " - " + y).blockingForEach(System.out::println);
A0 - B0
A1 - B0
A2 - B1
A3 - B1
A4 - B2
A5 - B3
A6 - B3
A7 - B4
A8 - B5
A9 - B5
```

The preceding code executes forever and needs to be manually stopped.

The merge operator

Merging multiple Observables into a single Observable with all the emissions from the all the given emissions can be achieved by calling:

- `merge`: Flattens the many input sources into one Observable, without any transformation
- `mergeArray`: Flattens the many input sources given as arrays into one Observable, without any transformation
- `mergeArrayDelayError`: Flattens the many input sources given as arrays into one Observable, without any transformation and without being interrupted by errors
- `mergeDelayError`: Flattens the many input sources into one Observable, without any transformation and without being interrupted by errors
- `mergeWith`: Flattens this and the given source into one Observable, without any transformation

In the following example, we will merge parts of the original 1 to 5 range in a way that it contains all the entries but in a different order:

```
jshell> io.reactivex.Observable.merge(
   ...>    io.reactivex.Observable.range(1, 5).skip(3),
   ...>    io.reactivex.Observable.range(1, 5).take(3)).
   ...>    subscribe(System.out::println);
4
5
1
2
3
$89 ==> DISPOSED
```

The zip operator

Combining multiple Observables into a single Observable based on a combiner function can be done by calling:

- `zip`: Emits the results of a specified combiner function applied to combinations of multiple items emitted by the given Observables

- `zipIterable`: Emits the results of a specified combiner function applied to combinations of multiple items emitted by the given Observables Iterable
- `zipWith`: Emits the results of a specified combiner function applied to combinations of this and the given Observable

The following code shows how `zip` can be applied to the elements emitted from a range of 1 to 5 to a range of 10 to 16 (more elements) based on string-concatenation combiner. Notice that the extra emission (number 16) does not get applied since there is no counterpart to be applied to:

```
jshell> io.reactivex.Observable.zip(
   ...>     io.reactivex.Observable.range(1, 5),
   ...>     io.reactivex.Observable.range(10, 16),
   ...>     (x, y) -> x + " - " + y).subscribe(System.out::println)
1 - 10
2 - 11
3 - 12
4 - 13
5 - 14
$90 ==> DISPOSED
```

Error handling

The Observables contain a couple of operators that allow error handling, swallowing exceptions, transforming exceptions, call-finally blocks, retrying the failed sequence, and disposing resources even if an error occurs.

The catch operator

These operators enable recovering from errors by continuing the sequence:

- `onErrorResumeNext`: Instructs an Observable to pass control to another Observable given by a supplier, instead of invoking `onError` when something goes wrong
- `onErrorReturn`: Instructs an Observable to emit a default supplied by a function, in case of error

- `onErrorReturnItem`: Instructs an Observable to emit a supplied default, in case of error
- `onExceptionResumeNext`: Instructs an Observable to pass control to another Observable instead of invoking `onError` in case something goes wrong

The following example shows how to use the `onErrorReturnItem` method; calling it without the `flatMap` trick will stop the flow and output `Default` at the end. By deferring the call to the exception-throwing code and applying `onErrorReturnItem` on it, we can continue the sequence and use the default supplied value:

```
jshell> io.reactivex.Observable.range(1, 5).
   ...>     flatMap(x ->  io.reactivex.Observable.defer(() ->
   ...>     {
   ...>     if (x != 3) {
   ...>        return io.reactivex.Observable.just("A"  + x);
   ...>     }
   ...>         else {
   ...>           throw new RuntimeException("Wrong value ");
   ...>     }}).
   ...> onErrorReturnItem("Default")).
   ...> subscribe(System.out::println);
A1
A2
Default
A4
A5
$91 ==> DISPOSED
```

The do operator

These are used to register an action to take upon a specific life cycle event. We can use them to mimic the final statement behavior, release resources allocated upstream, do performance measurements, or do other tasks that do not depend on the success of the current call. RxJava Observables enable this by providing the following methods:

- `doFinally`: Registers an action to be called when the current Observable invokes either `onComplete` or `onError` or gets disposed
- `doAfterTerminate`: Registers an action to be called after the current Observable invokes either `onComplete` or `onError`
- `doOnDispose`: Registers an action to be called when the sequence is disposed
- `doOnLifecycle`: Registers callbacks for the appropriate `onXXX` method, depending on the life cycle events of the sequence (subscription, cancellation, requesting)

- doOnTerminate: Registers an action to be called when the current Observable invokes either onComplete or onError

Following snippet shows usage of commands mentioned earlier:

```
jshell> io.reactivex.Observable<String> a = io.reactivex.Observable.just("a").
   ...>    doOnSubscribe(x -> System.out.println("OnSubscribe")).
   ...>    doOnTerminate(() -> System.out.println("OnTerminate")).
   ...>    doFinally(() -> System.out.println("OnFinally")).
   ...>    doOnComplete(() -> System.out.println("OnComplete")).
   ...>    doOnError(exch -> System.out.println("OnError"));
a ==> io.reactivex.internal.operators.observable.ObservableDoOnEach@35a50a4c

jshell> a.subscribe(System.out::println);
OnSubscribe
a
OnTerminate
OnComplete
OnFinally
$4 ==> DISPOSED
```

In the preceding example, we can see that the life cycle events order is: subscribe, terminate, complete, or error, and finally by registering a print to console action on each event.

The using operator

The using operator has a counterpart in Java called try-with-resources. It basically does the same—enables creating a disposable resource that gets released at a given time (when the Observable gets released). RxJava 2.0 method using implements this behavior.

The retry operator

These are operators to use in the case of a failure that is recoverable, such as a service that is temporarily down. They work by resubscribing in the hope that this time it will complete without error. The available RxJava methods are the following:

- retry: Replays the same flow in case of error forever until it succeeds
- retryUntil: Retries until the given stop function returns true
- retryWhen: Replays the same flow in case of error forever until it succeeds based on a retry logic function that receives the error/exception

In the following example, we use `zip` which contains only two values to create a retry logic that retries twice to run the failed sequence after a time period or 500 multiplied by the retry count. This approach can be used when connecting to non-responding web services, especially from mobile devices where each retry consumes the device battery:

```
jshell> io.reactivex.Observable.range(1, 5).
   ...>    map(x -> (x + 10) / (x - 5)).
   ...>    retryWhen(e -> e.zipWith(io.reactivex.Observable.range(1, 2), (x, y) -> y).
   ...>    flatMap(r -> io.reactivex.Observable.timer(500 * r, TimeUnit.MILLISECONDS))).
   ...>    subscribe(System.out::println);
-2
-4
-6
-14
$7 ==> 0

jshell> -2
-4
-6
-14
-2
-4
-6
-14

jshell>
```

Schedulers

Observables are agnostic in terms of thread scheduling–in a multithreading environment, this is the job of a scheduler. Some of the operators presented variants that can take a scheduler as a parameter. There are specific calls that allow observing the flow either from downstream (the point where the operator is used, this is the case of `observeOn`) or irrespective of call position (the call position does not matter, as this is the case of the `subscribeOn` method). In the following example, we will print the current thread from upstream and downstream. Notice that in the case of `subscribeOn`, the thread is always the same:

```
jshell> io.reactivex.Observable.range(1, 2).
   ...>    map(x -> {
   ...>      System.out.println("[Map]Thread " + Thread.currentThread().getName());
   ...>      return x + 10;
   ...>    }).
   ...>    observeOn(io.reactivex.schedulers.Schedulers.computation()).
   ...>    subscribe(y ->
   ...>      System.out.println("[Subscribe]Thread " + Thread.currentThread().getName() + " - " + y));
[Map]Thread main
[Map]Thread main
[Subscribe]Thread RxComputationThreadPool-5 - 11$10 ==> 3

jshell>
[Subscribe]Thread RxComputationThreadPool-5 - 12
```

Notice the thread main usage from the `map` method:

```
jshell> io.reactivex.Observable.range(1, 2).
   ...>    map(x -> {
   ...>      System.out.println("[Map]Thread " + Thread.currentThread().getName());
   ...>      return x + 10;
   ...>    }).
   ...>    subscribeOn(io.reactivex.schedulers.Schedulers.computation()).
   ...>    subscribe(y ->
   ...>      System.out.println("[Subscribe]Thread " + Thread.currentThread().getName() + " - " + y));
$11 ==> java.util.concurrent.ScheduledThreadPoolExecutor$ScheduledFutureTask@1ffe63b9

jshell> [Map]Thread RxComputationThreadPool-6
[Subscribe]Thread RxComputationThreadPool-6 - 11
[Map]Thread RxComputationThreadPool-6
[Subscribe]Thread RxComputationThreadPool-6 - 12

jshell>
```

Notice that the thread main is no longer used from the `map` method.

RxJava 2.0 offers more schedulers available from the
`io.reactivex.schedulers.Schedulers` factory, each one serving a specific purpose:

- `computation()`: Returns a `Scheduler` instance intended for computational work
- `io()`: Returns a `Scheduler` instance intended for I/O work
- `single()`: Returns a `Scheduler` instance for work requiring strongly-sequential execution on the same background thread
- `trampoline()`: Returns a `Scheduler` instance that executes the given work in a FIFO manner on one of the participating threads

- `newThread()`: Returns a `Scheduler` instance that creates a new thread for each unit of work
- `from(Executor executor)`: Converts `Executor` into a new `Scheduler` instance and delegates the work to it

There is a `Scheduler` only for special testing purpose, called `io.reactivex.schedulers.TestScheduler`. We have used it already since it allows manually advancing a virtual time, thus making it perfect for testing flows that are time-dependent without having to wait for the time to pass (for example, unit tests).

Subjects

Subjects are Observable and Subscriber hybrids since they both receive and emit events. There are five Subjects available in RxJava 2.0:

- `AsyncSubject`: Emits only the last value emitted by the source Observable followed by a completion
- `BehaviorSubject`: Emits the most recent emitted value and then any value emitted by the source Observable
- `PublishSubject`: Emits to a subscriber only those items that are emitted by the source after the time of the subscription
- `ReplaySubject`: Emits to any subscriber all of the items that were emitted by the source, even if there is no subscription
- `UnicastSubject`: Allows only a single Subscriber to subscribe to it during its lifetime

Example project

In the following example, we will show the usage of RxJava in the real-time processing of the temperature received from multiple sensors. The sensor data is provided (randomly generated) by a Spring Boot server. The server is configured to accept the sensor name as a configuration so that we may change it for each instance. We'll start five instances and display warnings on the client side if one of the sensors outputs more than 80 degrees Celsius.

Starting multiple sensors is easily done from bash with the following command:

```
$ for i in {1..5}
> do
> mvn spring-boot:run -Dserver.port=808$i -Dsensor.name=NuclearCell$i &
> done
[1] 4400
[2] 4344
[3] 1988
[4] 7028
[5] 8852
```

The server-side code is simple, we have only one REST controller configured to output the sensor data as JSON, as shown in the following code:

```
@RestController
publicclass SensorController
{
  @Value("${sensor.name}")
  private String sensorName;
  @RequestMapping(value="/sensor", method=RequestMethod.GET,
  produces=MediaType.APPLICATION_JSON_VALUE)
  public ResponseEntity<SensorData> sensor() throws Exception
  {
    SensorData data = new SensorData(sensorName);
    HttpHeaders headers = new HttpHeaders();
    headers.set(HttpHeaders.CONTENT_LENGTH, String.valueOf(new
    ObjectMapper().writeValueAsString(data).length()));
    returnnew ResponseEntity<SensorData>(data, headers,
    HttpStatus.CREATED);
  }
}
```

The sensor data is randomly generated in the `SensorData` constructor (notice the usage of the Lombock library to get rid of the setter/getter code):

```
@Data
publicclass SensorData
{
  @JsonProperty
  Double humidity;
  @JsonProperty
  Double temperature;
  @JsonProperty
  String sensorName;
  public SensorData(String sensorName)
```

```
    {
      this.sensorName = sensorName;
      humidity = Double.valueOf(20 + 80 * Math.random());
      temperature = Double.valueOf(80 + 20 * Math.random());
    }
  }
```

Now that we have our server started, we can connect to it from the RxJava-enabled client.

The client code makes use of the rxapache-http library:

```
publicclass Main
{
  @JsonIgnoreProperties(ignoreUnknown = true)
  staticclass SensorTemperature
  {
    Double temperature;
    String sensorName;
    public Double getTemperature()
    {
      return temperature;
    }
    publicvoid setTemperature(Double temperature)
    {
      this.temperature = temperature;
    }
    public String getSensorName()
    {
      return sensorName;
    }
    publicvoid setSensorName(String sensorName)
    {
      this.sensorName = sensorName;
    }
    @Override
    public String toString()
    {
      return sensorName + " temperature=" + temperature;
    }
  }
}
```

`SensorTemperature` is our client data. It is a snapshot of what the server can offer. The rest of the information is ignored by Jackson data binder:

```
publicstaticvoid main(String[] args) throws Exception
{
    final RequestConfig requestConfig = RequestConfig.custom()
    .setSocketTimeout(3000)
    .setConnectTimeout(500).build();
    final CloseableHttpAsyncClient httpClient = HttpAsyncClients.custom()
    .setDefaultRequestConfig(requestConfig)
    .setMaxConnPerRoute(20)
    .setMaxConnTotal(50)
    .build();
    httpClient.start();
```

In the preceding code, we set up and started the HTTP client by setting the TCP/IP timeouts and the number of connections allowed:

```
Observable.range(1, 5).map(x ->
Try.withCatch(() -> new URI("http", null, "127.0.0.1", 8080 + x, "/sensor",
null, null), URISyntaxException.class).orElse(null))
.flatMap(address ->
ObservableHttp.createRequest(HttpAsyncMethods.createGet(address),
httpClient)
.toObservable())
.flatMap(response -> response.getContent().map(bytes -> new String(bytes)))
.onErrorReturn(error -> "{\"temperature\":0,\"sensorName\":\"\"}")
.map(json ->
Try.withCatch(() -> new ObjectMapper().readValue(json,
SensorTemperature.class), Exception.class)
.orElse(new SensorTemperature()))
.repeatWhen(observable -> observable.delay(500, TimeUnit.MILLISECONDS))
.subscribeOn(Schedulers.io())
.subscribe(x -> {
if (x.getTemperature() > 90) {
System.out.println("Temperature warning for " + x.getSensorName());
} else {
System.out.println(x.toString());
}
}, Throwable::printStackTrace);
}
}
```

The preceding code creates a list of URLs based on a range, converts it to a list of responses, flattens the response bytes into a string, converts the string to JSON, and prints the result to the console. In the case of temperatures greater than 90, it will print a warning message. It does all this by running in the I/O Scheduler, repeatedly every 500 ms, and in case of errors, it returns default values. Notice the usage of Try monad, because the checked exceptions are thrown by the lambda code, that needs to be handled either by converting to an unchecked expression that can be handled by RxJava in `onError` or handle it locally in the lambda block.

Since the client spins forever, the partial output is as follows:

```
NuclearCell2 temperature=83.92902289170053
Temperature warning for NuclearCell1
Temperature warning for NuclearCell3
Temperature warning for NuclearCell4
NuclearCell5 temperature=84.23921169948811
Temperature warning for NuclearCell1
NuclearCell2 temperature=83.16267124851476
Temperature warning for NuclearCell3
NuclearCell4 temperature=81.34379085987851
Temperature warning for NuclearCell5
NuclearCell2 temperature=88.4133065761349
```

Summary

In this chapter, we learned about reactive programming and then focused on one of the most-used reactive libraries available–RxJava. We learned about reactive programming abstractions and their implementation in RxJava. We made the first steps into the RxJava world with concrete examples by understanding how Observables, schedulers, and subscriptions work, the most-used methods, and how are they used.

In the next chapter, we will learn about the most-used reactive programming patterns and how to apply them in our code.

7
Reactive Design Patterns

In the last chapter, we discussed the reactive programming style and highlighted the importance of going reactive. In this chapter, we will revisit the four pillars of reactive programming, namely responsive, resilient, elastic, and message-driven, one by one, and learn about the various patterns for implementing each of these pillars. We will cover the following topics in this chapter:

- Patterns for responsiveness
- Patterns for resilience
- Patterns for elasticity
- Patterns for message-driven communication

Patterns for responsiveness

Responsiveness means how interactive the application is. Does it interact with its users in a timely manner? Does clicking a button do what it is supposed to do? Does the interface get updated when it is meant to? The idea is that the application should not make the user wait unnecessarily and should provide immediate feedback.

Let's look at some of the core patterns that help us implement responsiveness in an application.

Request-response pattern

We will start with the simplest design pattern, the request-response pattern, which addresses the responsiveness pillar of reactive programming. This is one of the core patterns that we use in almost every application. It is our service that takes a request and returns a response. A lot of other patterns are directly or indirectly dependent on this, so it is worth spending a few minutes to understand this pattern.

The following diagram shows a simple request-response communication:

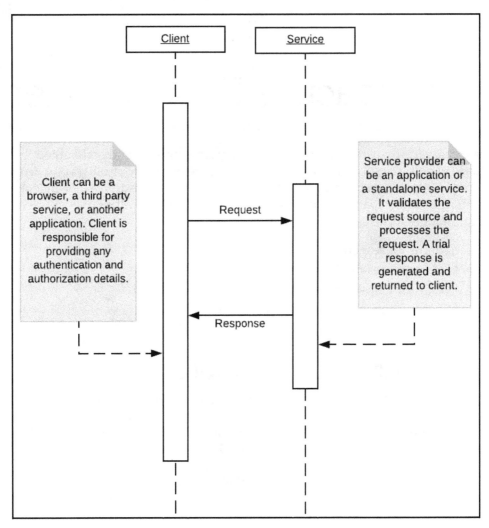

There are two parties to a request-response relationship. One entity makes a request and the second entity fulfills the request. A requester can be a browser asking for details from a server or a service asking for data from other service. Both parties need to agree upon the request and response formats. These can be in the form of XML, HTML, String, JSON, and so on; as long as both entities understand the communication, it is valid to use any format.

We will take a simple servlet-based example to start with. You might not be using a servlet-based implementation in real-world projects, unless you are working on a legacy application, yet it is important to understand the basics as they are the starting point for most of the modern-day frameworks we use.

We will create an employee service here that will handle GET and POST requests:

```java
/**
 *
 * This class is responsible for handling Employee Entity
   related requests.
 *
 */
public class EmployeeWebService extends HttpServlet
{
  public void init() throws ServletException
  {
    // Do required initialization
  }
  public void doGet(HttpServletRequest request,
  HttpServletResponse response) throws ServletException,
  IOException
  {
    // Set response content type
    response.setContentType("application/json");
    PrintWriter out = response.getWriter();
    /*
     * This is a dummy example where we are simply returning
    static employee details.
     * This is just to give an idea how simple request response
    works. In real world you might want to
     * fetch the data from data base and return employee list
    or an employee object based on employee id
     * sent by request. Well in real world you migth not want
    to use servlet at all.
     */
    JSONObject jsonObject = new JSONObject();
    jsonObject.put("EmployeeName", "Dave");
    jsonObject.put("EmployeeId", "1234");
    out.print(jsonObject);
    out.flush();
  }
  public void doPost(HttpServletRequest request,
  HttpServletResponse response) throws ServletException,
  IOException
  {
    // Similar to doGet, you might want to implement do post.
```

```
         where we will read Employee values and add to database.
    }
    public void destroy()
    {
        // Handle any object cleanup or connection closures here.
    }
}
```

The previous code should give you an idea of how a simple request-response pattern works. GET and POST are two of the most important types of communication available. GET, as the name suggests, is used to fetch any data, information, artifacts from the server, whereas POST adds new data to a server. About 10-12 years ago, you would have seen HTML embedded in servlets as well. But, of late, things have moved on to better and more maintainable designs. In order to maintain the separation of concerns and loose coupling, we try to keep our presentation layer, or frontend code, independent of our server-side code. This gives us freedom to create **application programming interfaces** (**API**) that can cater to a wide variety of clients, whether it be a desktop application, a mobile application, or a third-party-service-calling application.

Let's take it a step further and talk about RESTful services to maintain our APIs. **REST** stands for **Representational State Transfer**. The most common REST implementation is over HTTP, which is done by implementing GET, POST, PUT, and DELETE; that is, handling CRUD operations.

Let's take a look at these four core operations:

- GET: Fetches data as a list or single entity. Say we have an Employee entity: `<url>/employees/` will return a list of all the employees in the system. `<url>/employees/{id}/` will return a specific employee record.

- POST: Adds data for a new entity. `<url>/employees/` will add a new employee record to the system.

- PUT: Updates the data for an entity. `<url>/employees/{id}` will update an existing employee record in the system.

- DELETE: Deletes an existing entity record. `<url>/employees/{id}` will delete an existing employee record from the system.

As mentioned earlier, you will almost never write the explicit code to handle requests and responses directly. There are many frameworks, such as Struts, Spring, and so on, that help us avoid writing all the boilerplate code and focus on our core business logic.

Here is a quick Spring-based example; as you will see, we can avoid a lot of boilerplate code:

```
@RestController
@RequestMapping("/employees")
/**
* This class implements GET and POST methods for Employee Entity
*/
publicclass EmployeeWebService
{
  EmployeeDAO empDAO = new EmployeeDAO();
  /**
  * This method returns List of all the employees in the system.
  *
  * @return Employee List
  * @throws ServletException
  * @throws IOException
  */
  @RequestMapping(method = RequestMethod.GET)
  public List<Employee> EmployeeListService() throws
  ServletException, IOException
  {
    // fetch employee list and return
    List<Employee> empList = empDAO.getEmployeeList();
    return empList;
  }
  /**
  * This method returns details of a specific Employee.
  *
  * @return Employee
  * @throws ServletException
  * @throws IOException
  */
  @RequestMapping(method = RequestMethod.GET, value = "/{id}")
  public Employee EmployeeDataService(@PathVariable("id")
  String id) throws ServletException, IOException
  {
    // fetch employee details and return
    Employee emp = empDAO.getEmployee(id);
    return emp;
  }
  /**
  * This method returns Adds an Employee to the system
  *
  * @return Employee List
  * @throws ServletException
  * @throws IOException
```

```
  */
  @RequestMapping(method = RequestMethod.POST)
  public String EmployeeAddService(@RequestBody Employee emp)  throws
  ServletException, IOException
  {
    // add employee and return id
    String empId= empDAO.addEmployee(emp);
    return empId;
  }
}
```

As you can see, we are using a **Plain Old Java Object** (**POJO**) class and making it handle all our REST calls. There is no need to extend the `HttpServlet` or manage init or destroy methods.

If you are aware of Spring MVC, you can move onto the next pattern. For those who are new to the Spring framework, it's worth spending a few minutes to understand the working behind the previous example.

When you are using the Spring framework, you need to tell it about your server. So, in your `web.xml`, add the following:

```xml
<servlet>
  <servlet-name>springapp</servlet-name>
  <servlet-class>org.springframework.web.servlet.
  DispatcherServlet</servlet-class>
  <init-param>
    <param-name>contextClass</param-name>
    <param-value>org.springframework.web.context.support.
    AnnotationConfigWebApplicationContext </param-value>
  </init-param>
  <init-param>
    <param-name>contextConfigLocation</param-name>
    <param-value>com.employee.config.EmployeeConfig</param-value>
  </init-param>
  <load-on-startup>1</load-on-startup>
</servlet>
<servlet-mapping>
  <servlet-name>springapp</servlet-name>
  <url-pattern>/service/*</url-pattern>
 </servlet-mapping>
```

Here we have told `web.xml` that we are using Spring's dispatcher servlet, and any requests for pattern/service should be forwarded to our spring code. In addition to the previous code lines, we also need to provide spring with the configuration. This can be done in both Java-class-based or XML-based configurations. We have told `web.xml` to look for the configuration in `com.employee.config.EmployeeConfig`.

Here is a sample class-based configuration:

```
package com.employee.config;
import org.springframework.context.annotation.ComponentScan;
import org.springframework.context.annotation.Configuration;
import org.springframework.web.servlet.config.annotation.EnableWebMvc;
@EnableWebMvc
@Configuration
@ComponentScan(basePackages = "com.employee.*")
public class EmployeeConfig
{
}
```

As you can see, this is a very basic configuration file. You can also add database configurations, security aspects, and so on. Any further discussion on Spring MVC is out of scope for this book.

To run the previous code, we need to include certain JAR files for spring and other dependencies. These dependencies can be managed in different ways; for example, one might prefer adding Jars to repositories, or use Maven, Gradle, and so on. Again, a discussion of these tools is out of the scope of this book. Here are the dependencies that can be added to Maven for your benefit:

```
<dependencies>
  <dependency>
    <groupId>org.springframework</groupId>
    <artifactId>spring-webmvc</artifactId>
    <version>4.3.9.RELEASE</version>
  </dependency>
  <dependency>
    <groupId>javax.servlet</groupId>
    <artifactId>servlet-api</artifactId>
    <version>2.5</version>
    <scope>provided</scope>
  </dependency>
  <dependency>
    <groupId>com.fasterxml.jackson.core</groupId>
    <artifactId>jackson-databind</artifactId>
    <version>2.5.0</version>
  </dependency>
```

```
</dependencies>
```

Asynchronous-communication pattern

While we are discussing the responsive pillar of reactive programming, another important pattern one needs to consider is the asynchronous-communication pattern. While the request-response pattern makes sure that all the requests get successful responses, it does not take care of the fact that some of the requests might take a large amount of time to respond. The asynchronous-communication pattern helps our application to remain responsive, even if we are doing bulk tasks. The way we achieve responsiveness or quick responses is by making the core-task execution asynchronous. Think of it as your code requesting a service to do a certain task, say, updating the data in a database; the service receives the data and immediately responds that it has received the data. Note that the actual writing to the database has not been done yet, but a success message is returned to the calling method.

A more relevant example would be when a service is required to do a complex task, such as generating an Excel report by calculating the tax liability for each employee, which needs to be calculated on the fly, based on the salary and tax details provided by each employee. So, when the tax-reporting service receives a request to generate such a report, it will simply return a response acknowledging receipt of the request and the UI will show a message to refresh the page after a few minutes to see the updated report link. In this way, we are not blocking the end user, and he/she can do other tasks while the report is being generated at the backend.

Asynchronous communication is handled at multiple levels; for example, when a call is made to a server by a browser, our JavaScript frameworks, such as ReactJS or AngularJS, intelligently render the screen based on the amount of data received and asynchronously wait for data pending. But, here, we will focus more on Java-induced asynchronous communication. The simplest way to handle asynchronous tasks in Java is through threads.

Let's take an example. We have a scenario where we want to display an employee list on the UI, and, at the same time, compile a report with some complex calculations and send it to admin.

The following code shows how the code will look using the synchronous type of method calls:

```
/**
 * This method generates Employee data report and emails it to admin. This
 also
 * returns number of employees in the system currently.
```

```
*
* @return EmployeeCount
* @throws ServletException
* @throws IOException
*/
@RequestMapping(method = RequestMethod.GET, value = "/report")
public List<Employee> EmployeeReport() throws ServletException, IOException
{
  // Lets say this method gets all EmployeeDetails First
  List<Employee> empList = new EmployeeService().getEmployees();
  // Say there is a ReportUtil which takes the list data, does
  some calculations
  // and dumps the report at a specific location
  String reportPath = ReportUtil.generateReport();
  // Finally say we have an email service which picks the report
  and send to admin.
  EmailUtil.sendReport(reportPath);
  // Finally return the employee's count
  return empList;
}
```

Let's say fetching the data takes one second, generating the report takes four seconds, and emailing the report takes two seconds. We are making the user wait for seven seconds for his/her data. We can make the reporting asynchronous to make the communication faster:

```
/**
* This method generates Employee data report and emails it to admin. This
also
* returns number of employees in the system currently.
*
* @return EmployeeCount
* @throws ServletException
* @throws IOException
*/
@RequestMapping(method = RequestMethod.GET, value = "/report")
public List<Employee> EmployeeReport() throws ServletException, IOException
{
  // Lets say this method gets all EmployeeDetails First
  List<Employee> empList = new EmployeeService().getEmployees();
  Runnable myrunLambda = ()->
  {
    // Say there is a ReportUtil which takes the list data, does
    some calculations
    // and dumps the report at a specific location
    String reportPath = ReportUtil.generateReport();
    // Finally say we have an email service which picks the report
    and send to admin.
```

```
    EmailUtil.sendReport(reportPath);
};
new Thread(myrunLambda).start();
// Finally return the employee's count
return null;
}
```

We have moved the report generation and emailing parts out of the critical path, and the main thread now returns immediately after fetching the records. The reporting functionality is achieved in a separate thread. Other than threads, another important method of achieving asynchronous communication is with message queues and message-driven beans.

Caching pattern

Yet another pattern that may be used to make sure your application is responsive is to implement caching. Caching will make sure that similar types of requests are handled in a faster manner by caching the results. We can implement a cache at different levels, such as the controller level, service-layer level, data-layer level, and so on. We can also implement a cache before the request hits the code; that is, at the server or load-balancer level.

For the sake of this chapter, let's take a very simple example to see how caching helps us to improve performance. Let's take a simple webservice that returns data for an employee:

```
/**
 * This method fetches a particular employee data.
 * @param id
 * @return
 * @throws ServletException
 * @throws IOException
 */
@RequestMapping(method = RequestMethod.GET, value = "/{id}")
public Employee EmployeeDataService(@PathVariable("id") String id) throws
ServletException, IOException
{
    /*
     * Again, to keep it simple, returning a dummy record.
     */
    EmployeeService employeeService = new EmployeeService();
    Employee emp = employeeService.getEmployee(id);
    return emp;
}
```

This method fetches data from the database and returns it to the end user.

There are many cache implementations available in Java. For the sake of this example, let's create a very simple caching mechanism:

```
/**
 * A simple cache class holding data for Employees
 *
 */
class EmployeeCache
{
  static Map<String,Employee> cache = new HashMap<String,Employee>();
  /**
   * get Employee from cache
   * @param id
   * @return Employee
   */
  public static Employee getData(String id)
  {
    return cache.get(id);
  }
  /**
   * Set employee data to cache
   * @param id
   * @param employee
   */
  public static void putData(String id, Employee employee)
  {
    cache.put(id, employee);
  }
}
```

Now let's update our method to make use of caching:

```
/**
 * This method fetches a particular employee data.
 * @param id
 * @return
 * @throws ServletException
 * @throws IOException
 */
@RequestMapping(method = RequestMethod.GET, value = "/{id}")
public Employee EmployeeDataService(@PathVariable("id") String id) throws
ServletException, IOException
{
  /*
   * Lets check of the data is available in cache.
   * If not available, we will get the data from database and
```

```
   add to cache for future usage.
   */
   Employee emp = EmployeeCache.getData(id);
   if(emp==null)
   {
     EmployeeService employeeService = new EmployeeService();
     emp = employeeService.getEmployee(id);
     EmployeeCache.putData(id, emp);
   }
   return emp;
}
```

We can see the first time an employee's details are sought, they will not be found in the cache, and the normal flow for fetching data from the database will be executed. At the same time, this data is added to the cache. So, any subsequent requests to fetch data for the same employee would not need to hit the database.

Fan-out and quickest-reply pattern

In some applications, speed is very important, especially where real-time data is being handled, for example, on a betting site, where it is important to calculate the odds based on a live event. A goal scored in the last five minutes of time, for a match that was otherwise even, will dramatically change the odds in favor of a team, and you want this to be reflected on the website in a fraction of a second, before people start adding bets.

In such a case, where the speed of request handling is important, we would like multiple instances of the service to process the request. We will accept the response from the service that responded first, and discard other service requests. As you can see, this approach does guarantee speed, but it comes at a cost.

Fail-fast pattern

The fail-fast pattern states that if a service has to fail, it should fail fast and respond to calling entities as soon as possible. Think of this scenario: you have clicked a link and it shows you a loader. It makes you wait for three to four minutes and then shows an error message, **Service not available, please try again after 10 minutes.** Well, service not available is one thing, but why make someone wait just to tell them that the service is not available right now. In short, if a service has to fail, it should at least do it quickly to maintain a decent user experience.

One example of a fail-fast implementation is if your service is dependent on another service, you should have a quick mechanism to check if the third-party service is up or not. This can be done using a simple ping of the service. So, before sending an actual request and waiting for the response, we maintain health checks of the services. This is more important if our service is dependent on multiple services. It will be good to check the health of all the services before we start the actual processing. If any of the services are not available, our service will immediately send a response to wait, rather than partially processing the request and then sending a failure.

Patterns for resilience

When we are thinking about the resiliency of the application, we should try to answer the following questions: Can the application handle failure conditions? If one component of the application fails, does it bring down the whole application? Is there a single point of failure in the application?

Let's look at some patterns that will help us to make our application resilient.

The circuit-breaker pattern

This is an important pattern to implement both resilience and responsiveness in the system. Often, when a service fails in a system, it impacts other services as well. For example, service X calls service Y in the system to get or update some data. If service Y is unresponsive for some reason, our service X will make a call to service Y, wait for it to timeout, and then fail itself. Think of a scenario where service X itself is called up by another service P, and so on. We are looking at a cascading failure here, which will eventually bring down the whole system.

The circuit-breaker pattern, inspired by an electric circuit, suggests that, instead of letting the failure propagate, we should restrict the failure to a single service level; that is, we need a mechanism for service X to understand that service Y is unhealthy and the handle the situation. One way to handle the situation could be for service X to call service Y, and if it observes that service Y is not responding after N number of retries, it considers the service to be unhealthy and reports it to the monitoring system. At the same time, it stops making calls to service Y for a fixed amount of time (say, we set a 10-minute threshold).

Service X than gracefully handles this failure based on the importance of the actions performed by service Y. For example, if service Y is responsible for updating account details, service X will report a failure to the calling services, or for all services Y was performing to log the details of transactions, service X will add the logging details to a fallback queue, which can be cleared by service Y when it is back up.

The important factor here is not to let a single service failure bring down the whole system. Calling services should figure out which are the unhealthy services and manage a fallback approach.

Failure-handling pattern

Another important aspect for maintaining resilience in a system is asking the question, If one or more components or services go down, will my system still be able to function properly? For example, take an e-commerce site. There are many services and functionalities working together to keep the site up, such as product searches, product catalogs, recommendation engines, review components, the shopping cart, payment gateways, and so on. If one of the services, such as the search component, goes down due to load or hardware failure, will that impact end users' ability to place an order? Ideally, these two services should be created and maintained independently. So, if a search service is not available, the user can still place orders for items in the shopping cart or select items directly from the catalog and purchase them.

The second aspect of handling a failure is gracefully handling any requests to failed components. For the previous example, if a user tries to use the search functionality (say, the search box is still available on the UI), we should not show user a blank page or make him/her wait forever. We can show him/her the cached results or show a message that the service will be up in the next few minutes with recommended catalog.

Bounded-queue pattern

This pattern helps us maintain the resilience and responsiveness of the system. This pattern states that we should control the number of requests a service can handle. Most modern servers provide a request queue, which can be configured to let it know how many requests should be queued before requests are dropped and a server-busy message is sent back to the calling entity. We are extending this approach to the services level. Every service should be based on a queue, which will hold the requests to be served.

The queue should have a fixed size, which is the amount the service can handle in a specific amount of time, say, one minute. For example, if we know that service X can handle 500 requests in one minute, we should set the queue size to 500, and any other requests will be sent a message about the service being busy. Basically, we do not want the calling entities to wait for a long duration and impact the performance of the overall system.

Monitoring patterns

To maintain the resilience of the system, we need ways to monitor our services' performance and availability. There are multiple types of monitoring we can add to applications and services; for example, for responsiveness we can add a periodic ping to the application and validate how much time a response takes or we can check on the CPU and RAM usage of the system. If you are using a third-party cloud, such as **Amazon Web Services** (**AWS**), you get in built support for this kind of monitoring; otherwise one can write simple scripts to check the current state of health. Log monitoring is used to check whether errors or exceptions are being thrown in the application and how critical they are.

With monitoring in place, we can add alerting and automated error handling into the system. Alerting might mean sending email messages or text messages based on the severity of the problem. An escalation mechanism can also be built in; say, if the problem does not get solved in X amount of time, a message is sent to the next-level escalation point. By using automated error handling, we can make a call if additional instances of services need to be created, a service needs to be restarted, and so on.

Bulkhead pattern

Bulkhead is a term borrowed from cargo ships. In a cargo ship, the bulkhead is a wall built between different cargo sections, which makes sure that a fire or flood in one section is restricted to that section and other sections are not impacted. You've surely guessed what we are trying to suggest: failure in one service or a group of services should not bring down the whole application.

To implement the bulkhead pattern, we need to make sure that all our services work independently of each other and failure in one will not create a failure in another service. Techniques such as maintaining a single-responsibility pattern, an asynchronous-communication pattern, or fail-fast and failure-handling patterns help us to achieve the goal of stopping one failure propagating throughout the whole application.

Patterns for elasticity

An application must react to variable load conditions. If the load increases or decreases, the application should not be impacted and should be able to handle any load level without impacting the performance. One unmentioned aspect of elasticity is that your application should not use unnecessary resources. For example, if you expect your server to handle one thousand users per minute, you will not set up an infrastructure to handle ten thousand users as you will be paying 10 times the required cost. At the same time, you need to make sure that if the load increases, your application does not get choked.

Let's take a look at some of the important patterns that help us maintain the elasticity of the system.

Single responsibility pattern

Also known as the simple-component pattern or microservices pattern, the single-responsibility pattern is kind of an extension to the single-responsibility principle for OOP. We already discussed the single-responsibility principle in this book in the initial chapters. At a basic level, when applied to object-oriented programming, the single-responsibility principle states that a class should have only one reason to change. Taking that definition further to an architecture level, we broaden the scope of this principle to components or services. So now we are defining our single-responsibility pattern to mean that a component or service should be responsible for only a single task.

One needs to divide the application into smaller components or services, where each component is responsible for only one task. Dividing the service into smaller ones will result in microservices, which are easier to maintain, scale, and enhance.

To illustrate the point further, let's say we have a service called
`updateEmployeeSalaryAndTax`. This service takes the base salary and uses it to calculate
the total salary, including variable and fixed components, and, finally, calculates tax:

```
public void updateEmployeeSalaryAndTax(String employeeId, float baseSalary)
{
    /*
     * 1. Fetches Employee Data
     * 2. Fetches Employee Department Data
     * 3. Fetches Employee Salary Data
     * 4. Applies check like base salary cannot be less than existing
     * 5. Calculates House Rent Allowance, Grade pay, Bonus component
     based on Employees
     * position, department, year of experience etc.
     * 6. Updates Final salary Data
     * 7. Gets Tax slabs based on country
     * 8. Get state specific tax
     * 9. Get Employee Deductions
     * 10. Update Employee Tax details
     */
}
```

Though it looks logical to calculate this whenever a salary is updated, what if we only need
to calculate tax? Say, an employee updates tax-saving details, why do we need to calculate
all salary details again and not just update the tax data. A complex service not only
increases the execution time by adding unnecessary calculations but also hinders scalability
and maintainability. Say we need to update the tax formula, we will end up updating code
that has a salary calculation detail as well. The overall regression scope area increases.
Additionally, say we know salary updates are not common but tax calculations are updated
for every tax-saving-detail update, also the tax calculation is complex in nature. It might
have been easier for us to keep `SalaryUpdateService` on a smaller-capacity server and
`TaxCalculationService` on a separate, bigger machine, or have more than one instance
of `TaxCalculationService`.

A rule of thumb to check whether your service is doing exactly one task is to try to explain
it in plain English and look for the word `and`, for example, if we say this service updates
salary details `and` calculates tax, or this service modifies the data format `and` uploads it to
storage. The moment we see `and` in our explanation of the service, we know this can be
broken down further.

Stateless-services pattern

To make sure our services are scalable, we need to make sure we build them in a stateless manner. By stateless, we mean that the service does not retain any state from the previous calls and treats every request as a fresh, new one. The advantage this approach gives us is that we can easily create replicas of the same service and make sure it does not matter which service instance is handling the request.

For example, let's say we have ten instances of an `EmployeeDetails` service, which is responsible for serving me `<url>/employees/id`, and returning data for a specific employee. It does not matter which instance is serving the request, the user will always end up getting the same data. This helps us to maintain the elastic property of the system, as we can spin up any number of instances on the go and bring them down based on the load on the service at that point in time.

Let's look at a counter example; say we are trying to maintain the state of a user's actions using sessions or cookies. Here, the actions are performed on the `EmployeeDetails` service:

State 1: John has a successful login.

State 2: John has requested Dave's employee details.

State 3: John requests salary details, as he is on Dave's details page, and the system returns Dave's salary.

In this case, the *State 3* request does not mean anything unless we have the information from the previous state. We get a request `<url>/salary-details` and then we look at the session to understand who is asking for the details and for whom the request is being made. Well, maintaining the state is not a bad idea, but it can hinder scalability.

Say we see the load increasing for the `EmployeeDetail` service and plan to add a second server into the cluster. The challenge is that, say the first two requests went to Box 1 and the third request went to Box 2. Now Box 2 does not have a clue who is asking for salary details and for whom. There are solutions such as maintaining sticky sessions or copying sessions across the Boxes or keeping information in a common database. But these require additional work to be done and this defeats the purpose of quick autoscaling.

If we think of each request as independent—that is, self-sufficient in terms of providing the information being asked for, by whom, the current state of the user, and so on—we can stop worrying about maintaining the states of users.

For example, a simple change in request call from /salary-details to /employees/{id}/salary-details now provides information on whose details are being asked for. Regarding who is asking for the details—that is, authentication of the user—we can use techniques such as token-based authentication or sending a user token with a request.

Let's take a look at JWT-based authentication. **JWT** stands for **JSON Web Token**. JWT is nothing more than JSON embedded in a token or string.

Let's first look at how to create a JWT token:

```
/**
 * This method takes a user object and returns a token.
 * @param user
 * @param secret
 * @return
 */
public String createAccessJwtToken(User user, String secret)
{
  Date date = new Date();
  Calendar c = Calendar.getInstance();
  c.setTime(date);
  c.add(Calendar.DATE, 1);
  // Setting expiration for 1 day
  Date expiration = c.getTime();
  Claims claims = Jwts.claims().setSubject(user.getName())
  .setId(user.getId())
  .setIssuedAt(date)
  .setExpiration(expiration);
  // Setting custom role field
  claims.put("ROLE",user.getRole());
  return Jwts.builder().setClaims(claims).signWith
  (SignatureAlgorithm.HS512, secret).compact();
}
```

Similarly, we will write a method to take a token and get the details from token:

```
/**
 * This method takes a token and returns User Object.
 * @param token
 * @param secret
 * @return
 */
public User parseJwtToken(String token, String secret)
{
  Jws<Claims> jwsClaims ;
  jwsClaims = Jwts.parser()
```

```
       .setSigningKey(secret)
       .parseClaimsJws(token);
    String role = jwsClaims.getBody().get("ROLE", String.class);
    User user = new User();
    user.setId(jwsClaims.getBody().getId());
    user.setName(jwsClaims.getBody().getSubject());
    user.setRole(role);
    return user;
}
```

A complete discussion on JWT is out of scope for this book, but the previous code should help us to understand the basic concept of JWT. The idea is to add any critical information about the requesting entity in a token, so that we need not maintain a state explicitly. The token can be sent in the request as part of the params or header, and the servicing entity will parse the token to determine if the request is, indeed, coming from a valid party.

Autoscaling pattern

This is more of a deployment pattern than development pattern. But it is important to understand this, as it will impact our development practices. Autoscaling is directly related to the elastic property of the application. A service can be scaled up or down to handle a higher or lower number of requests in two ways: vertical scaling and horizontal scaling. Vertical scaling usually refers to adding more power to the same machine, and horizontal scaling refers to adding more instances that can load share. As vertical scaling is normally costly and has limits, when we talk about autoscaling we are usually referring to horizontal scaling.

Autoscaling is implemented by monitoring the instance-capacity usage and making a call based on that. For example, we can set a rule that whenever the average CPU usage of a cluster of instances that are hosting a service goes beyond 75%, a new instance should be booted to reduce the load on other instances. Similarly, we can have a rule that whenever the average load reduces below 40%, an instance is killed to save costs. Most of the cloud service providers, such as Amazon, provide inbuilt support for autoscaling.

Self-containment pattern

In simple words, self-containment means that an application or service should be self-sufficient or able to work as a standalone entity without depending on any other entity. Let's say we have a service for `EmployeeData` that tackles general employee data handling and another service for `EmployeeSalary`. Let's say we have given responsibility for maintaining database connections to the `EmployeeData` service. So, every time the `EmployeeSalary` service needs a database handled, it calls the `EmplyeeData` service's `getDatabaseHandle` method. This adds an unwanted dependency, which means that, unless the `EmployeeData` service is up and working fine, our `EmployeeSalary` service will not function properly. So, it is logical that the `EmployeeSalary` service should maintain its own database connection pool and operate in an autonomous manner.

Patterns for message-driven implementation

If we rely on message-based communication, we avoid tight coupling, enhance elasticity, as the components can grow or shrink without worrying about other components, and handle failure conditions, as one component's issues will not propagate to other components.

The following are the main design patterns one needs to be aware of when using reactive application programming.

Event-driven communication pattern

Event-driven communication is when two or more components message each other based on some event. An event can be adding new data, updating the data state, or removing data. For example, on addition of a new employee record to the system, an email needs to be sent to the manager. So the service or component responsible for managing employee records will message the component responsible for the emailing functionality on addition of a new record. There are multiple ways to handle this communication, but the most common method is through Message queues. The event-triggering component adds a message to the queue, and the receiver reads this message and performs its part of the action: in this case, sending an email to the manager.

The idea behind the event-driven pattern is that both the components are independent of each other, but, at the same time, can communicate with each other and take the required actions. In the previous example, the emailing component is independent of the component adding the record. If the emailing component is not able to process the request immediately, it will not impact the addition of the record. The emailing component might be under load or be down for some reason. When the emailing component is ready to process the message, it will read from the queue and performs the action is it required to do.

Publisher-subscriber pattern

Commonly known as the Pub-Sub pattern, this can be thought of as an extension to event-driven communication. In event-driven communication, one action triggers an event, on the basis of which another component needs to perform some action. What if multiple components are interested in listening to a message? What if the same component is interested in listening to multiple types of message? The problem is solved by using the concept of topics. In broader terms, we can think of an event as a topic.

Let's revisit the example where an employee-record addition event needs to trigger an email to the manager. Let's say there are other components, such as a transportation system, salary management system, and so on, which also need to perform some action based on the event that a new employee record is added. In addition, let's say that the emailing-the-manager component is also interested in events such as updating an employee record and deleting an employee record; in these cases, too, an email to the manager should also be triggered.

So, we have a topic called Employee Added, another for Employee Updated, and one for Employee Deleted. The component responsible for managing the employee data will publish all these events to queues, and hence is called a publisher. The components interested in one or more of these topics will subscribe to these topics, and are called subscribers. Subscribers will listen to the topics they are interested in and take action based on the message received.

The Pub-Sub pattern helps us implement loose coupling among components, as the subscriber need not be aware who the publisher is and vice versa.

Idempotency pattern

When we are aiming for message-driven and asynchronous communication, it can bring some challenges along. For example, if a duplicate message is added to the system, will it corrupt the state? Say we have a bank-account update service, and we send a message to add $1,000 to the account. What if we have a duplicate message? How will the system make sure it does not add the money twice just because a duplicate message is received? Also, how will this system differentiate between a duplicate message and a new message?

There are various techniques that can be used to handle to this problem. The most common is to add a message number or ID to each message, so the system can make sure that each message with a unique ID gets processed only once. Another way is to keep the previous state and new state in the message—say the old balance was X and the new balance is Y—and the system is responsible for applying the validation to make sure the state mentioned in the message (old balance) matches the system's state.

The bottom line is that, whenever we build a system, we need to make sure our application is able to take care of the scenario that a message sent repeatedly gets gracefully handled and does not corrupt the system's state.

Summary

In this chapter, we have talked about the patterns that help us maintain the reactive nature of an application, or, in other words, help us implement the four pillars of reactive programming, namely, responsiveness, resilience, elasticity, and message-driven communication.

In the next chapter, we will continue our journey and explore some contemporary aspects of a well-architected application.

8
Trends in Application Architecture

Whenever we start working on an application, the first thing we need to decide is the design or architecture we are going to use. As the software industry has matured in the last few decades, the way we used to design the systems has also changed. In this chapter, we will discuss some of the important architecture trends we have seen in the recent past and which are still relevant to date. We will try to analyze the good, the bad, and the ugly of these architectural patterns and figure out which pattern will be able to solve what type of problem. We will cover following topics in this chapter:

- What is application architecture?
- Layered architecture
- Model View Controller architecture
- Service-oriented architecture
- Microservices-based architecture
- Serverless architecture

What is application architecture?

When we start building an application, we have a set of requirements, and we try to design a solution that we feel will fulfill all the requirements. This design is known as **application architecture**. One important factor to consider is that your architecture should not only take care of current requirement, but should also anticipate expected future changes and take them into consideration. Quite often, there are some unspecified requirements, known as **non-functional requirements**, that you need to take care of. Functional requirements will be given as part of the requirements document, but architects or senior developers are expected to figure out non-functional requirements themselves. Performance needs, scalability needs, security requirements, maintainability, enhanceability, availability of applications, and so on, are some of the important non-functional requirements that need to be considered when architecting a solution.

The fact that makes the skill of application architecting both interesting and challenging is that there is no fixed set of rules. The architecture or design that worked for one application may not work for another; for example, a banking solution architecture may look different than an e-commerce solution architecture. Also, within one solution, different components may need to follow different design approaches. For example, you may want one of the components to support HTTP-REST based communication, whereas for another component, you may go for message queues for communication. The idea is to identify the best available approach for the current problem.

In the following sections, we will discuss some of the most common and effective architecting styles in JEE applications.

Layered architecture

We try to divide our code and implementation into different layers, and each layer will have a fixed responsibility. There is no fixed set of layering that can be applied to all the projects, so you may need to think about what kind of layering will work for the project in hand.

The following diagram shows a common layered architecture, which can be a good starting point when thinking about a typical web application:

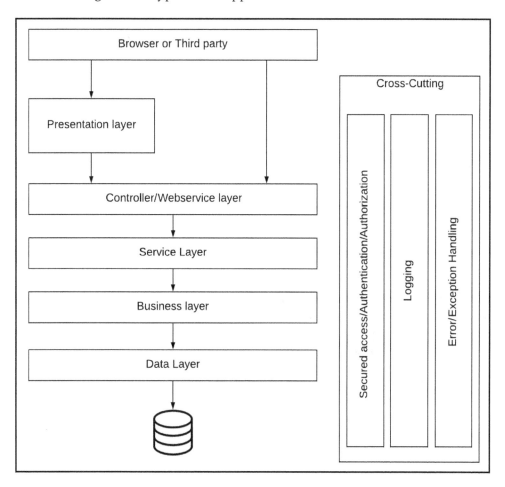

The design has the following layers:

- Presentation layer
- Controller/web service layer
- Service layer
- Business layer
- Data access layer

The **Presentation layer** is the layer that holds your UI, that is, HTML/JavaScript/JSPs, and so on. This is the layer that the end user can directly interact with.

The **Controller/web service layer** is the entry point for a request from a third party. This request can come from the presentation layer (mostly) or from another service; for example, a mobile or desktop application. As this is the entry point for any request, this layer will apply to any initial level checks, data cleanups, validations, security requirements, such as authentication and authorization, and so on. Once this layer is satisfied, the request is accepted and processed.

The **Service layer**, also known as the **application layer**, is responsible for providing different services, such as adding a record, sending emails, downloading a file, generating a report, and so on. In a small-scale application, we can merge the service layer with the web service layer, especially when we know that the service layer will only handle requests from the web. If the current service can be called from other services as well, it is better to keep the service separate from the web service or controller.

The **Business layer** holds all the business-related logic. For example, in an employee data management service, if the system is trying to promote an employee as manager, it is the responsibility of this layer to apply all the business checks, including whether the employee has relevant experience, whether they are already serving as a deputy manager, whether last year's appraisal rating matches with the required rules, and so on. Sometimes, if the application or service in question does not have a strong set of business rules, the business layer is merged with the application layer. On the other hand, you may want to further divide the business layer into sublayers in case your application demands strong implementation of business rules. Again, there is no fixed set of guidelines that you need to follow while implementing a layered design, and the implementation can change based on your application or service needs.

The **Data access layer** is the layer responsible for managing all data-related operations, such as fetching data, representing data in the required format, cleaning data, storing data, updating data, and so on. While creating this layer, we can use an **object relational mapping (ORM)** framework or create our own handlers. The idea here is to keep other layers free from worrying about data handling, that is, how data is being stored. Is it coming from another third-party service or being stored locally? These and similar concerns are the responsibility of this layer only.

Cross-cutting concerns are the concerns that each layer needs to handle; for example, each layer is responsible for checking whether the request is coming from the proper channel and no unauthorized request gets served. Each layer may want to record the entry and exit of a request by logging each message. These concerns can be handled through common utilities that are used and spread across the layers or can be handled by each layer independently. It is usually a good idea to keep these concerns independent of core business or application logic, using techniques such as **aspects-oriented programming (AOP)**.

Layered architecture with an example

To understand the layered architecture style further, let's take a look at the code and design example. Let's take a very simple requirement, where we need to get a list of employees from a database.

First of all, let's try to visualize the requirement in terms of layers by looking at this diagram:

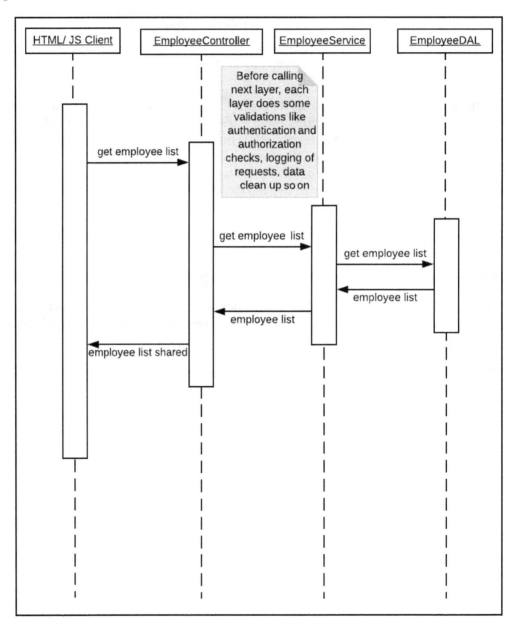

We have created four layers, in this case. The presentation layer can be thought of as a simple HTML with JavaScript. You may want to use sophisticated frameworks, such as ReactJS or AngularJS, to keep things organized at the presentation layer, but in this example we have a simple presentation layer, where, say, on clicking the **Show Employee List** button, an AJAX call is made to the controller layer, and the employee data is fetched.

Here is a simple JavaScript function that fetches the data for employees and displays it on the UI:

```
function getEmployeeData()
{
  var xhttp = new XMLHttpRequest();
  xhttp.onreadystatechange = function()
  {
    if (this.readyState == 4 && this.status == 200)
    {
      document.getElementById("demo").innerHTML = this.responseText;
    }
  };
  xhttp.open("GET", "/LayeredEmployeeExample/service/employees/", true);
  xhttp.send();
}
```

You can see that the presentation layer is not aware of the implementation of the next layer; all it is aware of is an API that should provide it with the required data.

Next, we move to the web service or controller layer. The responsibility of this layer is to make sure that requests are coming in the proper format and from the proper source. There are many frameworks available in Java, such as Spring Security and Java Web Token, which help us implement the authorization and authentication of each request. Additionally, we can create interceptors for this purpose. For the sake of keeping this chapter simple, we will focus on core functionality, that is, get data from the next layers and return it to the calling function. Take a look at this code:

```
/**
 * This method returns List of all the employees in the system.
 *
 * @return Employee List
 * @throws ServletException
 * @throws IOException
 */
@RequestMapping(method = RequestMethod.GET, value = "/")
public List<Employee> EmployeeListService() throws ServletException,
IOException
{
  List<Employee> empList = new ArrayList<Employee>();
```

```
    // Let's call Employee service which will return employee list
    EmployeeService empService = new EmployeeService();
    empList = empService.getEmployeeList();
    return empList;
}
```

Again, we can see that the current layer does not know who is calling it and does not know the implementation of the next layer.

Similarly, we have a service layer:

```
/**
 * This methods returns list of Employees
 * @return EmployeeList
 */
public List<Employee> getEmployeeList()
{
    // This method calls EmployeeDAL and gets employee List
    EmployeeDAL empDAL = new EmployeeDAL();
    return empDAL.getEmployeeList();
}
```

We have kept this layer ridiculously simple for the sake of this example. You could ask, why do we need an extra layer and not call the **data access layer** (**DAL**) from the controller itself? This can be done if you are sure that the only way to fetch employee data is through the controller. But we recommend having a service layer, as there will be cases when some other service needs to call our service, so we need not have duplicate business or DAL calls.

If you look closely, we have skipped the business layer. The idea is that you need not have all the layers just for sake of it. At the same time, you can break a layer into multiple layers or introduce new layers, based on the requirement in hand. In this case, we did not have any business rules to be implemented, so we have omitted the layer. On the other hand, if we wanted to implement some business rules, such as some of the employee records should be hidden from some specific roles, or they should be modified before being shown to the end user, we will implement a business layer.

Let's move on to our last layer here—the data-access layer. In our example, our DAL is responsible for fetching data and returning to the calling layer. Take a look at this code:

```
/**
 * This methods fetches employee list and returns to the caller.
 * @return EmployeeList
 */
public List<Employee> getEmployeeList()
{
    List<Employee> empList = new ArrayList<Employee>();
```

```
    // One will need to create a DB connection and fetch Employees
    // Or we can use ORM like hibernate or frameworks like mybatis
    ...
    return empList;
}
```

Tiers versus layers

In the real world, we see the words *tier* and *layer* being used interchangeably. For example, you must have heard the terms *presentation tier* or *presentation layer* referring to the same set of code. Though there is no harm in interchanging the terms when referring to a set of code, you need to understand that the term *tier* is used when we are dividing code based on physical deployment requirements, and layers are more concerned with logical segregation.

What does layered architecture guarantee?

Layered architecture guarantees us the following:

- **Code organization**: Layered architecture helps us implement code in a way in which each code layer is implemented independently. Code is more readable; for example, if you want to look at how particular data is accessed from a database, you can straightaway look at the DAL and ignore the other layers.
- **Ease of development**: As code is implemented in different layers, we can organize our teams in a similar way, where one team is working on the presentation layer and another on the DAL.

What are the challenges with layered architecture?

The challenges with layered architecture are as follows:

- **Deployment**: As the code is still somewhere tightly coupled, we cannot guarantee that we can deploy each layer independently of one another. We may still end up doing a monolithic deployment.
- **Scalability**: As we are still looking at the whole application as a monolithic deployment, we cannot scale components independently of one another.

Model View Controller architecture

Another widely used criteria for organizing code is by following the **Model View Controller** (**MVC**) architectural design pattern. As the name suggests, we are thinking about organizing our application into three parts, namely a model, a view, and a controller. Following MVC helps us maintain a separation of concerns and allows us to better organize our code. Take a look at the following:

- **Model**: A model is the representation of the data. Data is a critical part of any application. It is the responsibility of the model layer to organize and implement logic to manage and modify data properly. It takes care of any events that need to happen in case some data is modified. In short, the model has the core business implementation.

- **View**: Another important part for any application is the view, that is, the part with which the end user interacts. The view is responsible for displaying information to the end user and taking inputs from the user. This layer needs to make sure that the end user is able to get the intended functionality.

- **Controller**: As the name suggests, the controller controls the flow. When some action happens on the view, it will let the controller know, which in turn will take a call to determine whether this action impacts the model or the view.

As MVC is an old pattern, interpreted and used by architects and developers in a different manner, you may find different implementations of MVC patterns available. We will start with a very simplified implementation and then move to Java-specific implementations.

The following diagram gives us a basic understanding of the MVC flow:

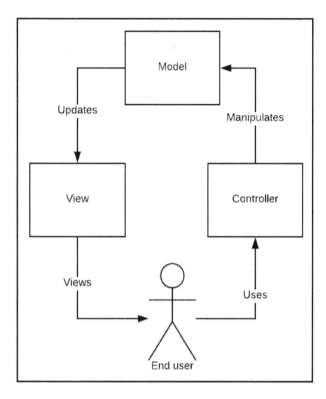

As we can see, the end user interacts with the controller in terms of an action, such as a form submission or a button click. The controller takes this request and updates data in the model. Finally, the view component gets updates based on the manipulation that has happened on the model. The updated view is rendered for the user to see and perform further actions.

As already mentioned, MVC is an old pattern, with its initial usage in desktop and static applications. The pattern has been interpreted and implemented differently by many web frameworks. In Java too, there are many frameworks providing web MVC implementation. Spring MVC is one of the most commonly used frameworks, so it is worth taking a look at.

The following diagram explains the flow of control in Spring MVC at a high level:

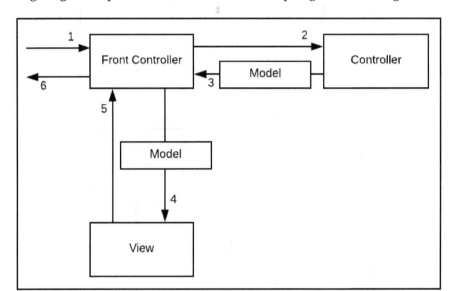

Let's take a closer look at the flow:

- **1**: Spring MVC follows the front controller pattern, which means that all the requests initially have to flow through a single point, in this case, a dispatcher servlet
- **2**: The front controller then delegates the request to the controller that is meant to handle the particular request
- **3**: The controller then manipulates or updates the model based on the given request, and returns the model requested by the end user
- **4**: The framework then selects the view that is meant to handle the current request and passes the model to it
- **5**: The view, generally JSPs, renders the data based on the model provided
- **6**: The final response, usually HTML, is sent back to the calling agent or browser

MVC architecture with an example

To clarify things further, let's look at a sample implementation. To start with, we will add the following to `web.xml`:

```xml
<servlet>
  <servlet-name>springmvc</servlet-name>
  <servlet-class>org.springframework.web.servlet.
  DispatcherServlet</servlet-class>
  <init-param>
    <param-name>contextClass</param-name>
    <param-value>org.springframework.web.context.support.
    AnnotationConfigWebApplicationContext</param-value>
  </init-param>
  <init-param>
    <param-name>contextConfigLocation</param-name>
    <param-value>com.employee.config.EmployeeConfig</param-value>
  </init-param>
  <load-on-startup>1</load-on-startup>
</servlet>
<servlet-mapping>
  <servlet-name>springmvc</servlet-name>
  <url-pattern>/mvc/*</url-pattern>
</servlet-mapping>
```

We have told our `web.xml` that all the requests with `/mvc/` pattern should be redirected to our front controller, that is, `DispatcherServlet` for Spring MVC. We have also mentioned the location of our configuration class file. This is our configuration file:

```java
@EnableWebMvc
@Configuration
@ComponentScan(basePackages = "com.employee.*")
/**
 * The main Configuration class file.
 */
public class EmployeeConfig
{
  @Bean
  /**
   * Configuration for view resolver
   */
  public ViewResolver viewResolver()
  {
    InternalResourceViewResolver viewResolver = new
    InternalResourceViewResolver();
    viewResolver.setViewClass(JstlView.class);
    viewResolver.setPrefix("/WEB-INF/pages/");
```

```
        viewResolver.setSuffix(".jsp");
        return viewResolver;
    }
}
```

We have told our application that we will be using the WebMVC framework and also the location of our components. In addition, we are letting the application know the location and format of our views through the view resolver.

Here is a sample controller class:

```
@Controller
@RequestMapping("/employees")
/**
* This class implements controller for Employee Entity
*/
public class EmployeeController
{
    /**
    * This method returns view to display all the employees in the system.
    *
    * @return Employee List
    * @throws ServletException
    * @throws IOException
    */
    @RequestMapping(method = RequestMethod.GET, value = "/")
    public ModelAndView getEmployeeList(ModelAndView modelView) throws
    ServletException, IOException
    {
        List<Employee> empList = new ArrayList<Employee>();
        EmployeeDAL empDAL = new EmployeeDAL();
        empList = empDAL.getEmployeeList();
        modelView.addObject("employeeList", empList);
        modelView.setViewName("employees");
        return modelView;
    }
}
```

We can see that this controller fetches the data in form of model, and lets the application know the appropriate view to respond to the current request. A `ModelAndView` object is returned, which has information about both the view and the model.

The controller gets passed to the view, which in this case is employees.jsp:

```
<%@ page language="java" contentType="text/html; charset=UTF-8"
pageEncoding="UTF-8" %>
<!DOCTYPE html PUBLIC "-//W3C//DTD HTML 4.01 Transitional//EN"
```

```
      "http://www.w3.org/TR/html4/loose.dtd">
      <html>
        <head>
          <meta http-equiv="Content-Type" content= text/html; charset=UTF-8">
          <title>Welcome to Spring</title>
          <%@ taglib uri="http://java.sun.com/jsp/jstl/core" prefix="c" %>
        </head>
        <body>
          <table>
            <th>Name</th>
            <th>Email</th>
            <th>Address</th>
            <th>Telephone</th>
            <th>Action</th>
            <c:forEach var="employee" items="${employeeList}">
              <tr>
                <td>${employee.id}</td>
                <td>${employee.name}</td>
                <td>${employee.designation}</td>
              </tr>
            </c:forEach>
          </table>
        </body>
      </html>
```

As we can see, all this view JSP is doing is to create an HTML that displays employee details in tabular form.

Spring MVC is more of a classical way of implementing MVC. In more recent times, we have tried to move away from JSPs to maintain separation of concerns. In modern applications, the view is normally independent of the server-side code and is completely rendered on the frontend using JavaScript frameworks such as ReactJS, AngularJS, and so on. Although the core principles of MVC still hold true, the communication may look different.

A more contemporary MVC implementation

For a rich internet application, the MVC implementation may look more like this diagram:

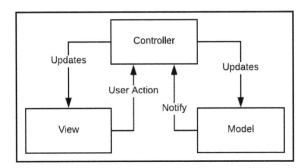

The core idea is that the model and view are completely independent. The controller receives communication from both the view and model and updates them based on the actions triggered. For example, when the user clicks a button on submit new employee record, the controller receives this request and in turn updates the model. Similarly, when a model gets updated, it notifies the controller, which then updates the view to reflect the correct model state.

What does MVC architecture guarantee?

MVC architecture guarantees the following:

- **Separation of concerns**: Similar to layered architecture, MVC guarantees a separation of concerns, that is, the view, model, and controller can be looked at as different components that need to be developed and maintained independently.
- **Ease of deployment**: There are different aspects of the application, that is, the model, view, and controller can be developed independently, by different teams. Although you would need to integrate these components to get the complete picture.

What are the challenges with MVC architecture?

The challenges with MVC architecture are as follows:

- **Scalability**: As we still need to deploy the whole application as a single unit, MVC cannot guarantee scalability. As we cannot scale only the parts relating to performance, the application needs to be scaled as a whole.
- **Testability**: The testability of the application is not straightforward with MVC. Although we can test one component independently, we need to integrate all the parts before we can test one functionality end to end.

Service-oriented architecture

When we talk about the **service-oriented architecture** (**SOA**) approach, we are talking about our application in terms of various services or reusable units. For example, let's take a look at an e-commerce shopping system, such as Amazon. It can be thought of as a combination of multiple services rather than a single application. We can think of a search service responsible for implementing a products search, a shopping cart service that will implement the maintenance of a shopping cart, a payment handling service that is independently handling payments, and so on. The idea is to break your application into services that can be developed, deployed, and maintained independently of one another.

To understand the advantage of the service-oriented architecture approach, let's consider a case where we are able to divide the application into 10 independent services. So, we have reduced the complexity of the architecture by 10 times. We are able to divide the team into 10 parts, and we know it is easier to maintain smaller teams. Also, it gives us freedom to architect, implement, deploy, and maintain each service independently. If we know that one particular service can be achieved better in one language or framework, whereas another service can be implemented in a totally different language or framework, we can do that easily. With independent deployment, we have the advantage of scaling each service independently based on its usage. Also, we can make sure that if one service is down or facing any issues, the other services are still able to respond without any issues. For example, if, for some reason, in an e-commerce system, we have an unresponsive search service, it should not impact the normal shopping cart and purchase feature.

Service-oriented architecture with an example

Suppose we are creating an employee management system that is responsible for creating, editing, and deleting record and, managing employee documents, leave plans, appraisals, transportation, and so on. Starting with this monolithic definition, let's start dividing it into different services. We will end up having a core `EmployeeRecordManagement` service, a `LeaveManagement` service, a `DocumentManagement` service, and so on. The very first advantage of this kind of breaking up into smaller services means we can design and develop these independently now. So the big 50-person team can be divided into 8-10 smaller, easy-to-manage teams, each owning its own service. We have loosely coupled services, which means making changes is also easier, as changing in leave rules does not mean you need to update the whole code. This kind of SOA approach also helps us with a phased delivery if required; for example, if I do not want to implement a leave management service right now, it can wait until the second release.

The following diagram should visually explain what an SOA design would like look for the preceding example:

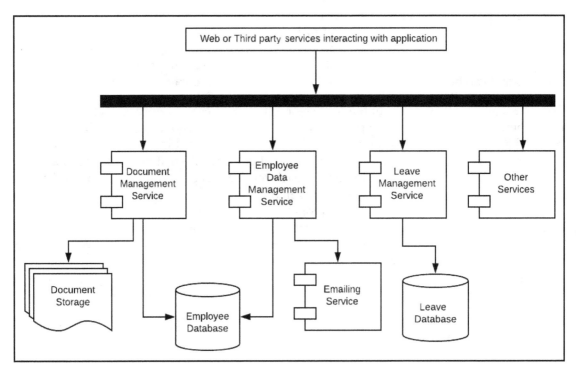

We can see that every service has an independent identity. But a service can interact with one another if required. Also, it is not uncommon for services to share resources, such as a database and storage.

For every service, we need to understand three core components:

- **Service provider**: The component that is providing the service. The service provider registers the services with the services directory.
- **Service consumer**: The component that is consuming the service. The service consumer can look for a service in the services directory.
- **Services directory**: The services directory contains a list of the services. It interacts with both the provider and the consumer to update and share services data.

Web services

Web services, as the name suggests, are services available over the web or the internet. Web services have helped popularize service-oriented architecture, as they have made it easy to think about an application in terms of services exposed over the internet. There are many ways to expose a service over the internet, **Simple Object Access Protocol** (**SOAP**) and REST being the two most common ways of implementation.

SOAP versus REST

Both SOAP and REST help in exposing services over the internet, but they are very different in nature.

A SOAP packet is XML based and needs to be in a very specific format. Here are the main components of a SOAP packet:

- **Envelope**: Identifies an XML packet as a SOAP message
- **Header**: Optional element to provide header information
- **Body**: Contains requests and responses for the service
- **Fault**: Optional element mentioning state and error

This is what a SOAP packet would look like:

```
<?xml version="1.0"?>
<soap:Envelope
xmlns:soap="http://www.w3.org/2003/05/soap-envelope/"
soap:encodingStyle="http://www.w3.org/2003/05/soap-encoding">
  <soap:Header>
    ...
  </soap:Header>
  <soap:Body>
    ...
    <soap:Fault>
      ...
    </soap:Fault>
  </soap:Body>
</soap:Envelope>
```

REST does not have so many rules and formats. A REST service can be implemented by supporting one or more of GET, POST, PUT, and DELETE methods over HTTP.

A sample JSON REST payload for a POST request would look like this:

```
{
  "employeeId":"1",
  "employeeName":"Dave",
  "department":"sales",
  ...
}
```

As we can see, there is no overhead, such as defining a proper packet structure, such as SOAP. Because of its simplicity, REST-based web services have become popular in the last few years.

Enterprise service bus

While we are discussing service-oriented architecture, it is important to understand what role **enterprise service bus** (**ESB**) can play to improve communication. You may end up creating several different services while developing different applications for your organization. At certain levels, these services need to interact with oen another. This can add a lot of complications. For example, one service understands XML-based communication, whereas another service expects all communication in JSON, and another service expects FTP-based input. Additionally, we need to add features such as security, queuing of requests, data cleanup, formatting, and so on. ESB is the solution to all our problems.

The following diagram shows how different services can communicate with ESB independently:

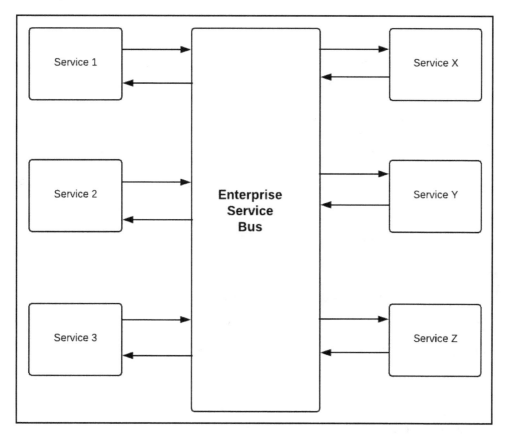

We can see that any number of services are interacting with ESB. One service may be written in Java, another in .Net, and others in other languages. Similarly, one service may expect a JSON-based packet, whereas another may need XML. It is the responsibility of ESB to make sure these services are interacting with one another smoothly. ESB also helps in service orchestration, that is we can control the sequencing and flow.

What does service-oriented architecture guarantee?

Service-oriented architecture guarantees the following:

- **Ease in development**: As we can divide the application into various services, it becomes easy for teams to work on different services without impacting one another work.
- **Loose coupling**: Each service is independent from the other, so if we change a service implementation, keeping the API request and response the same, the user need not know what has changed. For example, earlier, a service was fetching data from a database, but we introduced caching and made changes so that the service first fetches data from the cache. The caller services need not even know if something has changed within the service.
- **Testability**: Each service can be tested independently. Therefore, to test one service, you do not need to wait for the complete code to be ready.

What are the challenges with service-oriented architecture?

The challenges with service-oriented architecture are as follows:

- **Deployment**: Although we are thinking in terms of services, we are still architecting at the logical level and not considering independent deployment of these services. In the end, we may end up dealing with the deployment of a monolithic application that is difficult to enhance and maintain.
- **Scalability**: Scalability is still a major challenge with SOA. We are still dealing with larger services and mostly the service segregation is at the logical level and not at the physical level. So, scaling a single service or part of a service is tough. Most importantly, if we are using ESB, which itself is a large piece of deployment, scaling it can be a nightmare.

Microservices-based Architecture

Microservices-based architecture, as the name suggests, recommends dividing your services into a fine-grained level. There are different schools of thoughts when it comes to microservices; some will argue that it is just a fancy name for service-oriented architecture. We can definitely consider microservices as an extension of service-oriented architecture, but there are many features that make microservices different.

Micorservices take service-oriented architecture to the next level. SOA thinks of services at a feature level, whereas microservices take it to a task level. For example, if we have an email service for sending and receiving emails, we can have microservices such as a spell check, spam filter, and so on, each of which handles one specialized task.

An important differentiating factor that the concept of microservices brings in, with respect to SOA, is the fact that each microservice should be independently testable and deployable. Although these features are desirable with SOA, they become mandatory with microservices-based architecture.

Microservice architecture with an example

Let's look at a simple example to understand how microservices can help us. Let's say we need to build a feature on an e-commerce site, where you can upload pictures of products. When a product's image is uploaded, the service needs to save the image and also create a scaled version (suppose we want to keep all product images at a standard resolution of $1,280 \times 720$). In addition, we also need to create a thumbnail version of the image. In short, we are trying to do the following tasks in a single service.

The image upload service helps you to do the following:

1. Receive a product image.
2. Upload the image to storage.
3. Update the database with relevant information.
4. Scale the image to the standard resolution ($1,280 * 720$).
5. Upload the scaled image to storage.
6. Generate a thumbnail version of the image.
7. Upload the thumbnail to storage.
8. Return success.

Well, all the aforementioned tasks look important for a product image to be uploaded, but that looks like too much for the service. The microservices architecture can help us out in such scenarios. For example, we can rethink the service as the following microservices.

The image upload service helps you to do the following:

1. Receive a product image.
2. Upload the image to storage.
3. Update the database with relevant information.
4. Return success.

The scaled image service helps you to do the following:

1. Scale the image to the standard resolution (1,280*720).
2. Upload the scaled image to storage.

The thumbnail service helps you to do the following:

1. Generate a thumbnail version of the image.
2. Upload the thumbnail to storage.

You can still go ahead and create an upload to store service independently. So how fine-grained you want your services to be will depend on your system. Finding the right level of granularity is very important, as well as being a tricky task. If you do not properly break your bigger services into microservices, you will not be able to realize the advantages of microservices, such as scalability, ease of deployment, testability, and so on. On the other hand, if your microservices are too fine grained, you will unnecessarily end up maintaining too many services, which also means effort to make these services communicate with one another and handling-performance issues.

Communicating among services

Looking at the previous example, one obvious question that comes to mind is this: How would the scaled image service and thumbnail service be triggered? Well, there are many options. The most common ones are REST-based communication, where the upload service can make a REST call to the other two services, or message queue-based communication, where the upload service would add a message to the queue that can be processed by other services, or a state-based workflow, where the upload service will set a state in the database (for example, *ready for scaling*) that will be read by other services and processed.

Based on the application needs, you can take a call as to which communication method is preferred.

What does microservices-based architecture guarantee?

Microservices-based architecture guarantees the following:

- **Scalability**: One major challenge that we faced in all the previous architecture is scalability. Microservices help us to implement distributed architecture and hence support loose coupling. It is easier to scale these loosely coupled services, as each service can be deployed and scaled independently.
- **Continuous delivery**: In today's fast-paced needs of businesses, continuous delivery is an important aspect required by applications. As we are dealing with many services rather than a single monolithic application, it is much easier to modify and deploy a service as per requirements. In short, it is easy to push changes to production as one need not deploy the whole application.
- **Ease in deployment**: Microservices can be developed and deployed independently. So we do not need a bing bang deployment for the whole application; only the service effected can be deployed.
- **Testability**: Each service can be tested independently. If we have defined the request and response structure of each service properly, we can test the service as a standalone entity without worrying about other services.

What are challenges with microservices-based architecture?

The challenges with microservices-based architecture are as follows:

- **Dependency on devops**: As we need to maintain multiple services that are interacting with one another through messages, we need to make sure all the services are available and monitored properly.
- **Maintaining the balance**: Maintaining the right amount of microservices is a challenge in itself. If we have too fine-grained services, we have challenges such as deploying and maintaining too many services. On the other hand, if we have too few larger services, we will end up losing out on the advantages provided by microservices.
- **Repeated code**: As all our services are independently developed and deployed, some of the common utilities need to be copied to different services.

Serverless architecture

In all the architectural styles we have discussed so far, there is one common factor: dependency on the infrastructure. Whenever we are designing for an application, we need to think about important factors, such as these: How will the system scale up or scale down? How will the performance needs of the system be met? How will the services be deployed? How many instances and servers will we need? What will be their capacity? And so on.

These questions are important and at the same time tricky to answer. We have already moved from dedicated hardware to cloud-based deployments, which has eased our deployments, but still we need to plan for infrastructure requirements and answer all the aforementioned questions. Once hardware is acquired, whether on the cloud or otherwise, we need to maintain the health of it, and make sure that services are getting scaled based on their need, for which heavy devops involvement is required. Another important issue is underusage or overusage of the infrastructure. If you have a simple website, where you are not expecting too much traffic, you still need to provision some infrastructure capacity to handle the request. If you know you are expecting high traffic during only a few hours in the day, you need to intelligently manage your infrastructure to scale up and down.

To solve all the aforementioned problems, a completely new style of thinking has evolved, which is known as **serverless deployment**, or, in other words, providing functions as a service. The idea is that the development team should only worry about the code, and cloud service providers will take care of the infrastructure needs, including scaling of the functionalities.

What if you could pay only for the amount of computing power you use? What if you need not provision any infrastructure capacity beforehand? What if the service provider itself takes care of the scaling up of the computing capacity required, managing if there is a single request per hour or a million requests per second on its own?

Serverless architecture with an example

If we have got your attention already, let's take a very simple example to bring the point home. We will try to create a simple greetings example, where the function as a service implementation will greet the user. We will use the AWS Lambda function for this example.

Let's create our class with an example greeting function:

```
/**
 * Class to implement simple hello world example
 *
 */
public class LambdaMethodHandler implements RequestStreamHandler
{
  public void handleRequest(InputStream inputStream, OutputStream
  outputStream, Context context) throws IOException
  {
    BufferedReader reader = new BufferedReader(new InputStreamReader
    (inputStream));
    JSONObject responseJson = new JSONObject();
    String name = "Guest";
    String responseCode = "200";
    try
    {
      // First parse the request
      JSONParser parser = new JSONParser();
      JSONObject event = (JSONObject)parser.parse(reader);
      if (event.get("queryStringParameters") != null)
      {
        JSONObject queryStringParameters = (JSONObject)event.get
        ("queryStringParameters");
        if ( queryStringParameters.get("name") != null)
```

```
        {
          name = (String)queryStringParameters.get("name");
        }
      }
    }
    // Prepare the response. If name was provided use that
    else use default.
    String greeting = "Hello "+ name;
    JSONObject responseBody = new JSONObject();
    responseBody.put("message", greeting);
    JSONObject headerJson = new JSONObject();
    responseJson.put("isBase64Encoded", false);
    responseJson.put("statusCode", responseCode);
    responseJson.put("headers", headerJson);
    responseJson.put("body", responseBody.toString());
  }
  catch(ParseException parseException)
  {
    responseJson.put("statusCode", "400");
    responseJson.put("exception", parseException);
  }
  OutputStreamWriter writer = new OutputStreamWriter
  (outputStream, "UTF-8");
  writer.write(responseJson.toJSONString());
  writer.close();
  }
}
```

This simple function reads the input parameters from the query string and creates a greeting message, which is embedded into a *message* tag of JSON and returned to the caller. We will need to create a JAR file from this. If you are using maven, you could simply use a shade package such as *mvn clean package shade:shade*.

Once you have a JAR file ready, the next step is to create a Lambda function and upload the JAR. Go to your AWS account, choose **Lambda service** | **Create function** | **Author from scratch**, and provide the required values. Take a look at this screenshot:

You need to provide the **Name** and **Runtime** environment. Based on what your lambda function is supposed to do, you will be giving it permissions. For example, you may be reading from storage, accessing queues or databases, and so on.

Next, we upload the JAR file and save it to the lambda function, as shown in the following screenshot. Provide a fully qualified path for the handler function—`com.test.LambdaMethodHandler::handleRequest`:

Now, we test our function by setting a test event. Take a look at this screenshot:

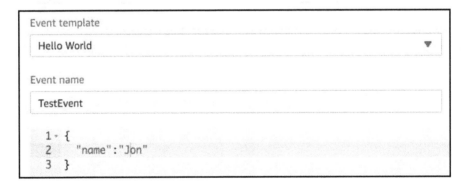

And, finally, clicking the **Test** button will show the response as follows:

```
{

    "isBase64Encoded": false,

    "headers": {},

    "body": "{"message":"Hello Guest"}",

    "statusCode": "200"
}
```

We have created a successful lambda function, but we need to understand how to call it. Let's create an API for calling this function. Amazon provides us with the API Gateway for this purpose. From **Designer**, under **Add triggers**, choose **API Gateway**, as shown in this screenshot:

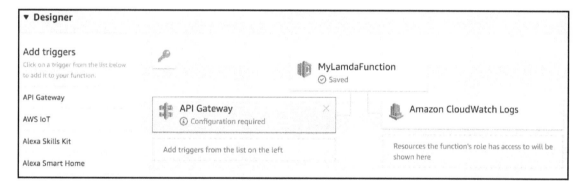

And, finally, add **API Gateway** configuration. Take a look at this screenshot:

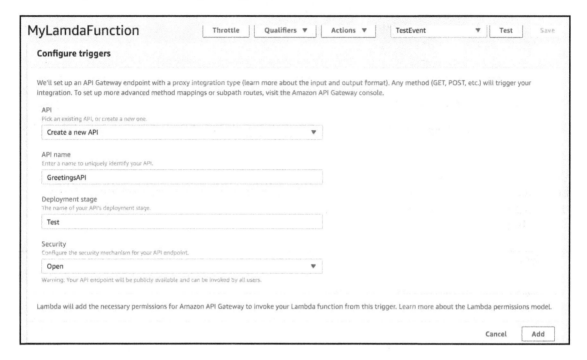

Once you add the configuration, you will be provided with an API link, which, when hit, will print the required JSON:

```
{"message":"Hello Guest"}
```

Or, if the name query parameter is provided, it will print `Hello {name}`.

Independence from infrastructure planning

One important and core idea of this whole exercise is to realize that we have created an API without setting up any machine or server. We simply created a JAR file and uploaded on Amazon. We are not worried about load or performance anymore. We don't think about whether we will use Tomcat or Jboss or any other server. We are not thinking about whether the API will get one hit or one million hits in a day. We will only pay for the number of requests and the computational power used.

Please note that we used the API to call the function and returned a simple message. Much more complex implementations are supported easily. For example, a function can be triggered from a message queue, database change, or storage and, similarly, can access other cloud provider services, such as a database, storage, messaging, emailing, and so on, along with third-party services.

Though we have used the Amazon Lambda example in this book, we do not recommend any specific vendor. The idea is to just explain the usage of serverless architecture. All the major cloud players, such as Microsoft, Google, IBM, and so on, provide their own implementation of serverless functions as service deployments. Readers are advised to choose as per their need and usage, after comparing their vendors of choice.

What does serverless architecture guarantee?

Serverless architecture guarantees the following:

- **Freedom from infrastructure planning**: Well, if not completely, up to a large extent, serverless architecture helps us focus on code and lets the service provider take care of the infrastructure. You need not think about scaling up and down your services and adding auto scaling or load-balancing logic.
- **Cost effective**: As you are paying only for the actual usage or actual traffic, you are not worried about maintaining minimum infrastructure levels. If your site is not getting any hit, you are not paying anything for the infrastructure (based on your cloud service provider conditions).
- **Next step up from microservices**: If you are already implementing microservices-based architecture, it will be an easy progression to serverless architecture. With function-based serverless implementation, it is easier to deploy a service implemented in the form a function.
- **Continuous delivery**: Like microservices, we can achieve continuous delivery with serverless architecture, as one function update will not impact the whole application.

What are the challenges with serverless architecture?

The challenges with serverless architecture are as follows:

- **Vendor-based limitation**: Various vendors can have limitations imposed when they provide functions as a service. For example, with Amazon, the maximum duration a server can execute for is five minutes. So, if you need to create a function that is doing heavy processing and can take more time than the limit imposed, Lambda functions may not be for you.
- **Managing distributed architecture**: Maintaining a large number of functions can get tricky. You need to keep a track of all the implemented functions and make sure an upgrade in one function API does not break other calling functions.

Summary

We talked about various architectural styles in this chapter, starting from layered architecture, MVC architecture, service-oriented architecture, microservices, and, finally, serverless architecture. One obvious question that comes to mind is: Which is the best among these styles of designing an application. The answer to this question is also pretty obvious—it depends on the problem at hand. Well, if there was one architecture that could apply to all the problems, everyone would have been using that, and we would have talked only about that particular architecture style.

An important thing to note here is that these architectural styles are not mutually exclusive; in fact, they complement one another. So, most of the time, you may end up using a hybrid of these architectural styles. For example, if we are working on a service-oriented architecture-based design, we may see that the internal implementation of these services may be done based on layered or MVC architectures. Also, we may end up breaking some of the services into microservices, and out of these microservices some may get implemented as a function in a serverless manner. The crux is, you will have to choose the design or the architecture based on the current problem you are trying to solve.

In the next chapter, we will focus on some of the latest trends and updates in recent Java version upgrades.

9
Best Practices in Java

In this chapter, we will talk about best practices in Java 9 and 10. Java has come a long way from Version 1.0, which was released in 1995 to the most recent version, Java 10. We will take a quick look at Java's journey from its inception to where it stands today, but we will focus more on recent changes brought in by Java 9 and 10.

In this chapter, we will cover the following topics:

- A brief history of Java
- Best practices and new features of Java 9
- Best practices and new features of Java 10

A brief history of Java

Java 1 was initially launched in 1995, and its Enterprise edition, or Java EE, was launched in 1999 with Java 2. Considering the fact that Java has been around for more than 20 years, there is no doubt that Java has what it takes to be the language of choice when it comes to building complex Enterprise applications.

Let's take a look at the features that made Java an instant hit:

- **Object-oriented**: Object-oriented languages are easy to learn, as they are closer to the real world. For developers already working with object-oriented languages, such as C++, it was easier to shift to Java, making it a popular choice.
- **Platform independent**: *Write once and execute anywhere* is the mantra for Java. As Java code is compiled into bytecode, which gets interpreted by JVM, there is no restriction on where to code and where to execute. We can develop a Java program on a Linux machine and run it on a Windows or macOS machine without any problem.

- **Security**: As Java code gets converted to bytecode, which runs within the **Java Virtual Machine (JVM)**, it is considered secure, as it cannot access any memory outside JVM. Additionally, Java does not support pointers, and memory management is completely the responsibility of JVM, making the language secure.

Along with core Java, what popularized the language further was the introduction of concepts such as servlets with J2EE. The internet was getting popular, and with the ease of use and security features provided by Java, it became an important language in web application development. Further concepts, such as multithreading, helped in achieving better performance and resource management.

Java 1.2 was called Java 2 because of the major changes it brought along in the form of the Enterprise edition. Java 2 was so popular that the next two versions, 1.3 and 1.4, were popularly known as Java 2 versions only. Then came Java 5, which brought along some important features and, it was given an independent identity.

Features of Java 5

Java 5 brought generics into the picture. Before generics, many of the data structures, such as Lists and Maps, were not typesafe. That is, you could have added a person and a vehicle into the same list and then tried to perform actions, which could result in errors.

Another important feature brought in by Java 5 was autoboxing, which helps the conversion between primitive type classes and corresponding wrapper classes. Enums, too, got a new life with Java 5. They could not only keep constant values, but could keep data and behavior as well.

Methods were provided with varargs. You were no longer forced to give the exact number of elements if they were of the same type. For example, you could simply write stringMethod(String... str) and pass any number of strings to this method. Java 5 also introduced annotations, which were enhanced in later versions, and became an integral part of many frameworks.

There were many other enhancements in Java 5, which made the release an important point in the history of Java.

After Java 5, Java 6 and 7 were other important versions, but major changes were brought along by Java 8.

Features of Java 8

Java 8 is another important milestone release in the history of Java. Along with many other features, such as opening interfaces for the first time to allow static and default method definition, the `optional` and `forEach` were introduced; the two core additions are streams and Lambda expressions.

Streams can be thought of as pipelines of data, in which we can perform two types of operations: intermediate and terminal. Intermediate operations are the ones that are applied on the stream to transform data, but the result is still a stream; for example, `map` and `filter`. For example, in a stream of integer data, with an apply function such as filter out all even numbers or add N to each number, we end up having a resultant stream. Whereas, terminal operations result in concrete output. For example, the sum function on a stream of integer data will return a final number as the output.

With Lambda expressions, Java has its first encounter with functional programming. Lambdas help us implement functional interfaces, which are interfaces with a single unimplemented method. Unlike older versions where we had to create a class or anonymous class, we can now create a Lambda function to implement a functional interface. A classic example is runnable to implement multithreading. Take a look at this code:

```
Runnable myrunnable = new Runnable()
{
  @Override
  public void run()
  {
    // implement code here
  }
};
new Thread(myrunnable).start();
But with Lambdas, we can do this:
Runnable myrunnableLambda = ()->
{
  // implement code here
};
new Thread(myrunnableLambda).start();
```

We have covered some details on streams and lambdas already in `Chapter 5`, *Functional Patterns*.

Currently supported versions of Java

At the time of writing this book, two versions are officially supported by Oracle for Java. These are Java 8 and Java 10. Java 8 is the long-term support version, and Java 10 is the rapid-release version. Java 9 was another rapid-release version, released in September 2017, and stopped receiving updates from January 2018. Java 8 was released in March 2014, and is expected to have commercial support until January 2019 and non-commercial support until December 2020. Java 10 was released in March 2018 and an expected end of life in September 2018. At the same time, when Java 10 is going out of support, we expect Java 11 to be released, which will be another long-term support version such as Java 8.

As we can see, Java 9 and 10 are the more recent versions, so it makes sense to understand all the new features they have brought in and some of the best practices when using these new versions.

Best practices and new features of Java 9

The most important and biggest change brought along by Java 9 is the implementation of Project Jigsaw or the Java platform module system. Before this change, you would need the complete **Java Runtime Environment** (**JRE**) as a whole to be loaded on a server or a machine to run a Java application. With Project Jigsaw, you can decide what libraries need to be loaded for an application. Apart from the module system, Java 9 also added jshell to Java's arsenal, a boon for people who have worked in languages such as Ruby on Rails, Python, and so on. This comes with similar features. We will discuss modules and Jshell in detail, along with a few other significant changes brought by Java 9, which impact how we code in Java.

Java platform module system

If Java 8 helped us change the way we were coding, Java 9 is more about how files and modules are loaded when an application runs.

To get started, let's see how Java 9 has divided the whole application into modules. All you need to do is run this code:

```
java --list-modules
```

You will see a module list similar to the one in the following screenshot:

```
java.activation@9.0.4
java.base@9.0.4
java.compiler@9.0.4
java.corba@9.0.4
java.datatransfer@9.0.4
java.desktop@9.0.4
java.instrument@9.0.4
java.jnlp@9.0.4
java.logging@9.0.4
java.management@9.0.4
java.management.rmi@9.0.4
java.naming@9.0.4
java.prefs@9.0.4
java.rmi@9.0.4
java.scripting@9.0.4
java.se@9.0.4
java.se.ee@9.0.4
java.security.jgss@9.0.4
java.security.sasl@9.0.4
java.smartcardio@9.0.4
java.sql@9.0.4
java.sql.rowset@9.0.4
java.transaction@9.0.4
java.xml@9.0.4
java.xml.bind@9.0.4
java.xml.crypto@9.0.4
java.xml.ws@9.0.4
java.xml.ws.annotation@9.0.4
javafx.base@9.0.4
javafx.controls@9.0.4
javafx.deploy@9.0.4
javafx.fxml@9.0.4
javafx.graphics@9.0.4
javafx.media@9.0.4
javafx.swing@9.0.4
javafx.web@9.0.4
jdk.accessibility@9.0.4
jdk.aot@9.0.4
jdk.attach@9.0.4
jdk.charsets@9.0.4
jdk.compiler@9.0.4
jdk.crypto.cryptoki@9.0.4
jdk.crypto.ec@9.0.4
jdk.deploy@9.0.4
jdk.deploy.controlpanel@9.0.4
jdk.dynalink@9.0.4
jdk.editpad@9.0.4
jdk.hotspot.agent@9.0.4
jdk.httpserver@9.0.4
jdk.incubator.httpclient@9.0.4
jdk.internal.ed@9.0.4
jdk.internal.jvmstat@9.0.4
jdk.internal.le@9.0.4
jdk.internal.opt@9.0.4
jdk.internal.vm.ci@9.0.4
```

The advantage we have now is that we can choose which modules will be used by our application instead of adding all the modules by default.

To understand the power of modules, let's look at an example. Let's try to create a very simple calculator application that provides just add and subtract methods, to keep it simple.

Let's create the class in provider/com.example/com/example/calc:

```
package com.example.calc;
/**
* This class implements calculating functions on integers.
*/
public class Calculator
{
  /**
  * This method adds two numbers.
  */
  public int add(int num1, int num2)
  {
    return num1+num2;
  }
  /**
  * This method returns difference between two numbers.
  */
  public int diff(int num1, int num2)
  {
    return num1-num2;
  }
}
```

Now let's create a module—info.java in provider/com.example:

```
module com.example
{
  requires java.base;
  exports com.example.calc;
}
```

We need not provide requires java.base explicitly. It will be added by default, as all the modules are requires java.base by default. But we have kept it just to be explicit.

Now compile the classes:

```
javac -d output/classes provider/com.example/module-info.java
provider/com.example/com/example/calc/Calculator.java
```

And, finally, create the JAR:

```
jar cvf output/lib/example.jar -C output/classes/
```

So, we have a module ready that can serve add and subtract functionality. Let's see how to use this module by creating a user class in
`user/com.example.user/com/example/user`:

```
package com.example.user;
import com.example.calc.*;
/**
 * This classes uses calculator module
 */
public class User
{
  public static void main(String s[])
  {
    Calculator calculator = new Calculator();
    System.out.println(calculator.add(1,2));
  }
}
```

Again, we will need to create module—`info.java` in `user/com.example.user`:

```
module com.example.user
{
  requires com.example;
}
```

Let's compile the methods, this time into `output/userclasses`:

```
javac --module-path output/lib -d output/userclasses
user/com.example.user/module-info.java
user/com.example.user/com/example/user/User.java
```

Create `user.jar`, as shown here:

```
jar cvf output/lib/user.jar -C output/userclasses/
```

Finally, run the class:

```
java --module-path output/lib -m com.example.user/com.example.user.User
```

The preceding code explains how modules work in Java 9. Before moving on to the next topic, let's take a look at jlink, which adds power to Java modularization:

```
jlink --module-path output/lib --add-modules com.example,com.example.user -
-output calculaterjre
```

Please note that you will need to add `java.base.mod` to `/output/lib`, as our `com.example` is dependent on the `java.base` module. Once you are able to create your custom JRE, you can run it as the following:

```
./calculaterjre/bin/java -m com.example.user/com.example.user.User
```

You can see that we are able to create our own little JRE. To get an idea of how compact and lightweight our little executable is, let's run `--list-modules` again:

```
calculaterjre/bin/java --list-modules w
```

This returns the following:

```
com.example
com.example.user
java.base@9.0.4
```

Compare it to the modules that we listed initially that came with Java 9 by default. We can get an idea of how lightweight our new deployable unit is.

JShell

We have already given some examples of JShell usage previously in this book. Here, we will take a more descriptive view of JShell. If you have worked in languages, such as Python or Ruby on Rails, you must have noticed the cool shell feature or **Read-Eval-Print Loop** (**REPL**) tool. The idea is to try out and experiment with the language before you go and do the real implementation. It was about time that Java added a similar feature to it.

Jshell is an easy way to get started with Java. You can write code snippets, see how they work, look at the behavior of different classes and methods without actually writing complete code, and play around with Java. Let's take a closer look to get a better understanding.

Let's start the shell first. Note Java 9 is a prerequisite and `jdk-9/bin/` should have been added to your system path.

Just type `jshell` and it will take you to the jshell prompt with a welcome message:

```
$ jshell
| Welcome to JShell -- Version 9.0.4
| For an introduction type: /help intro
jshell>
```

Let's try out a few simple commands to get started:

```
jshell> System.out.println("Hello World")
 Hello World
```

A simple `Hello World`. There is no need to write, compile, or run the class:

```
jshell> 1+2
$1 ==> 3
jshell> $1
$1 ==> 3
```

When we type `1+2` in the shell, we get the result in a variable: `$1`. Note that we can use this variable in later commands:

```
jshell> int num1=10
num1 ==> 1
jshell> int num2=20
num2 ==> 2
jshell> int num3=num1+num2
num3 ==> 30
```

In the preceding commands, we created a couple of variables and used those later.

Let's say I want to try out a code to see how it will work in a real application. I can do that with the shell. Suppose I want to write a method and try it out, to assess if it is returning the expected results and whether it will fail under certain circumstances. I can do all that in the shell as follows:

```
jshell> public int sum(int a, int b){
...> return a+b;
...> }
| created method sum(int,int)
jshell> sum(3,4)
$2 ==> 7
jshell> sum("str1",6)
| Error:
| incompatible types: java.lang.String cannot be converted to int
| sum("str1",6)
| ^----^
```

I created a method and saw how it will behave with different inputs.

You can also use JShell as a tutorial, to learn all the functions that are available for an object.

For example, suppose I have a `String str`, and I want to know about all the methods that are available for this. All I need to do is write `str` and press *Tab*:

```
jshell> String str = "hello"
str ==> "hello"
jshell> str.
```

The output is as follows:

```
jshell> String str = "hello"
str ==> "hello"

jshell> str.
charAt(                 chars()                 codePointAt(            codePointBefore(        codePointCount(         codePoints()
compareTo(              compareToIgnoreCase(    concat(                 contains(               contentEquals(          endsWith(
equals(                 equalsIgnoreCase(       getBytes(               getChars(               getClass()              hashCode()
indexOf(                intern()                isEmpty()               lastIndexOf(            length()                matches(
notify()                notifyAll()             offsetByCodePoints(     regionMatches(          replace(                replaceAll(
replaceFirst(           split(                  startsWith(             subSequence(            substring(              toCharArray()
toLowerCase(            toString()              toUpperCase(            trim()                  wait(
```

There are additional help commands provided by jshell. The first one you may want to use is `/help` to give you all the commands. Another useful command is `/import` to check all the packages that are already imported:

```
jshell> /import
|    import java.io.*
|    import java.math.*
|    import java.net.*
|    import java.nio.file.*
|    import java.util.*
|    import java.util.concurrent.*
|    import java.util.function.*
|    import java.util.prefs.*
|    import java.util.regex.*
|    import java.util.stream.*
```

You can import additional packages and classes to the shell and use them.

Finally, /exit will let you close the shell:

```
jshell> /exit
| Goodbye
```

Private methods in interfaces

Java 8 allowed us to add default and static methods to interfaces, where you were required to implement only unimplemented methods in the interface. Now, as we are allowed to add default implementations, it may be possible that we want to break our code into modules or pull out common code in a method that can be used by other functions. But we do not want to expose this common method. To solve this, Java 9 has allowed private methods in interfaces.

The following code shows a perfectly valid implementation of an interface in Java 9, which has a helper private method used by a default method:

```
package com.example;
/**
 * An Interface to showcase that private methods are allowed
 *
 */
public interface InterfaceExample
{
  /**
   * Private method which sums up 2 numbers
   * @param a
   * @param b
   * @return
   */
  private int sum(int a, int b)
  {
    return a+b;
  }
  /**
   * Default public implementation uses private method
   * @param num1
   * @param num2
   * @return
   */
  default public int getSum(int num1, int num2)
  {
    return sum(num1, num2);
  }
  /**
```

```
 * Unimplemented method to be implemented by class which
   implements this interface
   */
   public void unimplementedMethod();
}
```

Enhancements in streams

Java 8 brought us the wonderful feature of streams, which has helped operations on lists and sets of data very easily and efficiently. Java 9 has further enhanced the usage of streams to make them more useful. Here we will discuss important enhancements in streams:

- **Takewhile**: Java 8 gave us a filter that would check each element against a filter condition. For example, suppose from a stream we need all numbers less than 20. There may be a case where we want the list of all the numbers before we meet the condition and ignore the rest of the input. That is, when the first time filter condition is breached, ignore the rest of the input, and something such as the return or exit command is executed.

  The following code showcases the case where all numbers are returned unless the condition that the number is less than 20 is met. All the data after the condition is met once is ignored:

  ```
  jshell> List<Integer> numList = Arrays.asList(10, 13, 14, 19, 22,
  19, 12, 13)
  numList ==> [10, 13, 14, 19, 22, 19, 12, 13]
  jshell> numList.stream().takeWhile(num -> num <
  20).forEach(System.out::println)
  ```

  The output is as follows:

  ```
  10
  13
  14
  19
  ```

- **Dropwhile**: This is almost a reverse of `takewhile()`. Dropwhile makes sure to drop all the inputs unless a given condition is met and after the condition is met once, all the data is reported as output.

  Let's take the same example as takewhile to make things clear:

  ```
  jshell> List<Integer> numList = Arrays.asList(10, 13, 14, 19, 22,
  19, 12, 13)
  ```

```
numList ==> [10, 13, 14, 19, 22, 19, 12, 13]
jshell> numList.stream().dropWhile(num -> num <
20).forEach(System.out::println)
```

The output is as follows:

```
22
19
12
13
```

- **Iterate**: Java 8 already had support for `Stream.iterate`, but with Java 9 we can add a predicate condition, making it closer to a loop with a terminating condition.

  The following code shows a replacement of the loop condition that has a variable initiated to 0, incremented by 2, and printed until the number is less than 10:

  ```
  jshell> IntStream.iterate(0, num -> num<10, num ->
  num+2).forEach(System.out::println)
  ```

  The output is as follows:

  ```
  0
  2
  4
  6
  8
  ```

Creating immutable collections

Java 9 gives us factory methods to create immutable collections. For example, to create an immutable list, we use List.of:

```
jshell> List immutableList = List.of("This", "is", "a", "List")
immutableList ==> [This, is, a, List]
jshell> immutableList.add("something")
| Warning:
| unchecked call to add(E) as a member of the raw type java.util.List
| immutableList.add("something")
| ^---------------------------^
| java.lang.UnsupportedOperationException thrown:
| at ImmutableCollections.uoe (ImmutableCollections.java:71)
| at ImmutableCollections$AbstractImmutableList.add
(ImmutableCollections.java:77)
| at (#6:1)
```

Similarly, we have `Set.of`, `Map.of`, and `Map.ofEntries`. Let's take a look at the usage:

```
jshell> Set immutableSet = Set.of(1,2,3,4,5);
immutableSet ==> [1, 5, 4, 3, 2]
jshell> Map immutableMap = Map.of(1,"Val1",2,"Val2",3,"Val3")
immutableMap ==> {3=Val3, 2=Val2, 1=Val1}
jshell> Map immutableMap = Map.ofEntries(new
AbstractMap.SimpleEntry<>(1,"Val1"), new
AbstractMap.SimpleEntry<>(2,"Val2"))
immutableMap ==> {2=Val2, 1=Val1}
```

Method addition in arrays

We have talked about streams and collections so far. There are a few additions to arrays as well:

- **Mismatch**: This tries to match two arrays and returns the index of the first element where the arrays mismatch. It returns −1 if both arrays are the same:

```
jshell> int[] arr1={1,2,3,4}
arr1 ==> int[4] { 1, 2, 3, 4 }
jshell> Arrays.mismatch(arr1, new int[]{1,2})
$14 ==> 2
jshell> Arrays.mismatch(arr1, new int[]{1,2,3,4})
$15 ==> -1
```

We created an integer array. The first comparison shows that the array mismatched at index 2. The second comparison shows that both arrays are the same.

- **Compare**: This compares two arrays lexicographically. You can also specify start and end indexes, which is an optional argument:

```
jshell> int[] arr1={1,2,3,4}
arr1 ==> int[4] { 1, 2, 3, 4 }
jshell> int[] arr2={1,2,5,6}
arr2 ==> int[4] { 1, 2, 5, 6 }
jshell> Arrays.compare(arr1,arr2)
$18 ==> -1
jshell> Arrays.compare(arr2,arr1)
$19 ==> 1
jshell> Arrays.compare(arr2,0,1,arr1,0,1)
$20 ==> 0
```

We created two arrays and compared them. When both arrays are equal, we will get 0 output. If the first one is larger lexicographically, we will get 1; otherwise, we will get −1. In the last comparison, we provided start and end indexes of arrays to be compared. So, only the first two elements were compared for both arrays, which were equal, and hence 0 was the output.

- **Equals**: As the name suggests, the equals method checks whether the two arrays are equal. Again, you can provide start and end indexes:

```
jshell> int[] arr1={1,2,3,4}
arr1 ==> int[4] { 1, 2, 3, 4 }
jshell> int[] arr2={1,2,5,6}
arr2 ==> int[4] { 1, 2, 5, 6 }
jshell> Arrays.equals(arr1, arr2)
$23 ==> false
jshell> Arrays.equals(arr1,0,1, arr2,0,1)
$24 ==> true
```

Additions to the Optional class

Java 8 gave us the `java.util.Optional` class to handle null values and null pointer exceptions. Java 9 added a few more methods:

- `ifPresentOrElse`: The method `void ifPresentOrElse(Consumer<? super T> action, Runnable emptyAction)` performs the given action if the `Optional` value is present; otherwise, `emptyAction` is performed. Let's take a look at a few examples:

```
//Example 1
jshell> Optional<String> opt1= Optional.ofNullable("Val")
opt1 ==> Optional[Val]
//Example 2
jshell> Optional<String> opt2= Optional.ofNullable(null)
opt2 ==> Optional.empty
//Example 3
jshell> opt1.ifPresentOrElse(v->System.out.println("found:"+v),
()->System.out.println("no"))
found:Val
//Example 4
jshell> opt2.ifPresentOrElse(v->System.out.println("found:"+v),
()->System.out.println("not found"))
not found
```

- **Or**: As the Optional object can have a value or null, the or function helps in a case when you need to return the current Optional object if it has some legit value or else return some other Optional object.

Let's take a look at a few examples:

```
//Example 1
jshell> Optional<String> opt1 = Optional.ofNullable("Val")
opt1 ==> Optional[Val]
//Example 2
jshell> Optional<String> opt2 = Optional.ofNullable(null)
opt2 ==> Optional.empty
//Example 3
jshell> Optional<String> opt3 = Optional.ofNullable("AnotherVal")
opt3 ==> Optional[AnotherVal]
//Example 4
jshell> opt1.or(()->opt3)
$41 ==> Optional[Val]
//Example 5
jshell> opt2.or(()->opt3)
$42 ==> Optional[AnotherVal]
```

As opt1 is not null, it is returned when used with or; whereas opt2 is null, and hence opt3 is returned.

- **Stream**: Streams have become popular after Java 8, so Java 9 gives us a method to convert an Optional object to streams. Let's take a look at a few examples:

```
//Example 1
jshell> Optional<List> optList =
Optional.of(Arrays.asList(1,2,3,4))
optList ==> Optional[[1, 2, 3, 4]]
//Example 2
jshell> optList.stream().forEach(i->System.out.println(i))
[1, 2, 3, 4]
```

New HTTP client

Java 9 brings a new sleek HTTP client API with HTTP/2 support. Let's take a closer look by running an example in jshell.

To use httpclient, we need to start jshell with the jdk.incubator.httpclient module. The following command tells jshell to add the required module:

```
jshell -v --add-modules jdk.incubator.httpclient
```

Now lets import the API:

```
jshell> import jdk.incubator.http.*;
```

Create an `HttpClient` object using the following code:

```
jshell> HttpClient httpClient = HttpClient.newHttpClient();
httpClient ==> jdk.incubator.http.HttpClientImpl@6385cb26
| created variable httpClient : HttpClient
```

Let's create a request object for a URL https://www.packtpub.com/:

```
jshell> HttpRequest httpRequest = HttpRequest.newBuilder().uri(new
URI("https://www.packtpub.com/")).GET().build();
httpRequest ==> https://www.packtpub.com/ GET
| created variable httpRequest : HttpRequest
```

Finally, make the call to the URL. The result will be stored in the `HttpResponse` object:

```
jshell> HttpResponse<String> httpResponse = httpClient.send(httpRequest,
HttpResponse.BodyHandler.asString());
httpResponse ==> jdk.incubator.http.HttpResponseImpl@70325e14
| created variable httpResponse : HttpResponse<String>
```

We can check the response status code and even print the body:

```
jshell> System.out.println(httpResponse.statusCode());
200
jshell> System.out.println(httpResponse.body());
```

We can see how easy it is to use and there is no need to include heavy third-party libraries for HTTP clients.

Some more additions to Java 9

So far, we have discussed the core additions to Java 9 that will impact your day-to-day coding life. Let's take a look at some more feature additions, which may not have that big an impact but are still good to know about:

- **Improvement in Javadocs**: Java 9 brings in improvements in Javadocs, such as support for HTML 5, the addition of search capabilities, and the addition of module information to existing Javadocs functionality.

- **Multi-release JAR**: Suppose you have different versions of a class that should run on different Java versions. For example, Java has two different versions, one you know will support Java 8 and another for Java 9. You will create both class files and include them while creating the JAR file. The correct version of the file will be picked based on the JAR that is being used with Java 7 or Java 9.

- **Process API improvements**: Java 5 gave us the Process Builder API, which helps in spawning new processes. Java 9 brings in `java.lang.ProcessHandle` and `java.lang.ProcessHandle.Info` APIs for better control and for gathering more information about the processes.

- **Try with resources improvements**: Java 7 brought in a feature where you could use a try block to manage resources and help in removing a lot of boilerplate code. Java 9 has further improved it so that you need not introduce a new variable in the try block to use try with the resources.

  Let's take a look at a small example to understand what we mean. The following is the code that you would have written before Java 9:

```
jshell> void beforeJava9() throws IOException{
...> BufferedReader reader1 = new BufferedReader(new
FileReader("/Users/kamalmeetsingh/test.txt"));
...> try (BufferedReader reader2 = reader1) {
...> System.out.println(reader2.readLine());
...> }
...> }
| created method beforeJava9()
```

  The code after Java 9 is as follows:

```
jshell> void afterJava9() throws IOException{
...> BufferedReader reader1 = new BufferedReader(new
FileReader("/Users/kamalmeetsingh/test.txt"));
...> try (reader1) {
...> System.out.println(reader1.readLine());
...> }
...> }
| created method afterJava9()
```

- **Diamond operator with anonymous classes**: Up to Java 8, you could not have used a diamond operator with inner classes. This restriction is removed in Java 9.

We have covered most of the important features of Java 9 that will impact the way you code in Java. Using the aforementioned practices will help us utilize Java's capabilities to the fullest. But we know there are additional changes that are brought about by Java 10, so in the next section we will discuss some of the important features that impact our code further.

Best practices and new features of Java 10

Java 10 is the latest and current version for Java. Like previous versions, this too brings in some interesting feature additions to the language. Some features we will be able to interact with directly when we code, but there are other improvements that work behind the scenes, such as improved garbage collection, which improves the overall experience of users. In this section, we will discuss some of the important features added by Java 10.

Local variable type inference

This is probably the biggest change in Java 10 that will impact the way you used to code. Java is always known as a strict type language. Well, it still is, but with Java 10 you have the liberty of using `var` when declaring local variables instead of providing proper type.

Here is an example:

```
public static void main(String s[])
{
  var num = 10;
  var str = "This is a String";
  var dbl = 10.01;
  var lst = new ArrayList<Integer>();
  System.out.println("num:"+num);
  System.out.println("str:"+str);
  System.out.println("dbl:"+dbl);
  System.out.println("lst:"+lst);
}
```

We are able to define and use variables without specifying the type. But this feature is not without its set of restrictions.

You cannot declare a class scope variable as `var`. For example, following code will show a compiler error:

```
public class VarExample {
// not allowed
```

```
// var classnum=10;
}
```

Even in the local scope, var can be used only if a compiler can infer the type of the variable from right-hand side of the expression. For example, the following is fine:

```
int[] arr = {1,2,3};
```

However, this is not fine:

```
var arr = {1,2,3};
```

However, you can always use the following:

```
var arr = new int[]{1,2,3};
```

There are other situations where you cannot use `var`. For example, you cannot define the method return type or method arguments with var.

The following is not allowed:

```
public var sum(int num1, int num2)
{
    return num1+num2;
}
```

This is not allowed either:

```
public int sum(var num1, var num2)
{
    return num1+num2;
}
```

Even though you can use var to declare your variables with var, a word of caution is necessary. You need to be careful how you are declaring your variable to maintain the readability of the code. For example, you may come across this line in your code:

```
var sample = sample();
```

Can you make out anything about this variable sample? Is it a string or an integer? You could argue that we can give a proper naming convention while naming our variables, such as strSample or intSample. But what if your type is a bit complex? Take a look at this:

```
public static HashMap<Integer, HashMap<String, String>> sample()
{
    return new HashMap<Integer, HashMap<String, String>>();
}
```

In this case, you may want to make sure you are using a proper type-based declaration to avoid code readability concerns.

Another area where you need to be careful when declaring collections is `ArrayLists`. For example, this is now legitimate in Java:

```
var list = new ArrayList<>();
list.add(1);
list.add("str");
```

You can very well see the problem here. The compiler has inferred the preceding list containing *objects*, whereas your code may be looking for a list of integers. So we are expecting some serious runtime errors in such cases. So, it is better to always be explicit in such cases.

So, in short, `var` is a great addition to Java and can help us code faster but we need to be careful while using it to avoid code readability and maintenance issues.

copyOf method for collections

The `copyOf` method is introduced to create an unmodifiable copy of collections. For example, suppose you have a list and you need an immutable or unmodifiable copy, you can use the `copyOf` function. If you have used collections, you may wonder how it is different than `Collections.unmodifiableCollection`, which promises to do the same thing, that is create an unmodifiable copy of the collection. Well, although both methods give us an unmodifiable copy, when we use `copyOf` on a collection, say a list, it returns a list that cannot further be modified plus any changes to the original list do not impact the copied list. On the other hand, `Collections.unmodifiableCollection` does return an unmodifiable list in the aforementioned case, but this list will still reflect any modifications in the original list.

Let's take a closer look to make things clearer:

```
public static void main(String args[]) {
List<Integer> list = new ArrayList<Integer>();
list.add(1);
list.add(2);
list.add(3);
System.out.println(list);
var list2 = List.copyOf(list);
System.out.println(list2);
var list3 = Collections.unmodifiableCollection(list);
System.out.println(list3);
```

```
// this will give an error
// list2.add(4);
// but this is fine
list.add(4);
System.out.println(list);
// Print original list i.e. 1, 2, 3, 4
System.out.println(list2);
// Does not show added 4 and prints 1, 2, 3
System.out.println(list3);
// Does show added 4 and prints 1, 2, 3, 4
}
```

Similarly, we can use the `copyOf` function for sets, hashmaps, and so on, to create an unmodifiable copy of the objects.

Parallelization of full garbage collection

In languages such as C and C++, it was the developer's responsibility to allocate and de-allocate the memory. This can be tricky because if the developer makes a mistake, such as forgetting to deallocate an allocated piece of memory, it can cause an out of memory issue. Java handled this problem by providing garbage collection. The responsibility of allocating and deallocating the memory is moved from the developer to Java.

Java maintains its memory using two mechanisms: the stack and heap. You must have seen two different errors, namely `StackOverFlowError` and `OutOfMemoryError`, representing the fact when one of the memory areas is full. Memory in the stack is visible only to the current thread. Thus the cleanup is straightforward; that is, when the thread leaves the current method, the memory on the stack gets released. Memory in the heap is trickier to manage as it can be used throughout the application; hence, specialized garbage collection is required.

Over the years, Java has improved **garbage collection** (**GC**) algorithms to make them more and more effective. The core idea is that if a memory space allocated to an object is not getting referenced anymore, the space can be freed up. Most of the GC algorithms divide memory allocated into young generation and old generation. From usage, Java was able to mark that most of the objects become eligible for GC early on or during the initial GC cycle. For example, objects defined in a method are active only until the method is active and once the response is returned, the local scope variable becomes eligible for GC.

The G1 collector, or garbage-first garbage collector, was first introduced in Java 7 and was made default in Java 9. The garbage collection is mainly done in two phases. In phase one, the garbage collector marks the elements that can be removed or cleaned; that is, they are no longer referenced. The second phase actually cleans the memory. Also, these phases run independently on different units with different generations of memory allocated. The G1 collector can do most of the activities concurrently behind the scenes without stopping the application, except the full garbage collection. The full garbage collection is needed when partial GCs that usually clean younger generation memory are not sufficiently cleaning the space.

With Java 10, the full garbage collection can be done by parallel threads. This was done earlier in a single threaded mode. This improves the overall GC performance when it comes to full GC.

Some more additions to Java 10

We have covered most of important feature additions to Java 10, but there are a few more that are worth discussing here:

- **Time-based release versioning**: Well, this is not exactly a new feature, but more of the way Java has recommended how it will be versioning future releases. If you are in Java for the long term, it is worth understanding how Java versions are being released.

  The release number is in the following format:
  `$FEATURE.$INTERIM.$UPDATE.$PATCH`

  Java has decided to release a new feature version every six months. Keeping this in mind, the Java 11 release is scheduled in September 2018, six months after Java 10 was released. The idea is to keep getting the latest changes every six months. There are two schools of thought; one supporting this arrangement, as users will get changes frequently, but a second group says it will give developers less time to get accustomed to a release.

So, if you look at a release number 10.0.2.1, you know this belongs to feature release 10, with no interim release, update release 2, and patch 1.

- **Graal compiler**: The compiler is a computer program that takes the code as input and converts it to machine language. Java's JIT compilers convert the code to bytecode, which then gets converted to machine language by a JVM. With Java 10, you can use the experimental Graal compiler on a Linux machine. A point to note is that this is still in the experimental stage and is not recommended for production.

- **Application class data sharing**: This is another internal update to Java, so you may not notice it while coding, but it is good to know about it. The idea is to reduce the startup time for a Java application. A JVM loads classes on application startup. If you do not update your files, earlier JVM would still reload all the classes. With Java 10, JVM will create this data once and add it to an archive, and if the classes are not updated next time, it will need not reload the data. Also, if multiple JVMs are running, this data can be shared across them. Again, this update is not a visible one but will improve the overall performance of the applications.

We have covered most of the important features of Java 10 so far. Before closing this chapter, let's take a look at what the future has in store for Java; that is, what can be expected from Java 11 and when is it scheduled for release?

What should be expected in Java 11?

Java 11 is expected to be released somewhere around September 2018. It is worth taking a look at some of the important features expected in Java 11:

- **Local variable syntax for Lambda expression**: Java 10 brought in a feature where we can use var while declaring the local variables, but it is not allowed to be used with Lambda expression right now. This restriction is supposed to go away with Java 11.

- **Epsilon-low overhead garbage collector**: This JEP or JDK enhancement proposal talks about implementing a *no-op* garbage collector. In other words, this garbage collector is supposed to mainly focus on memory allocation and not implement any memory reclamation mechanism. It may be hard to imagine an application that does not need any garbage collections, but this is targeted at a set of applications that do not allocate too much heap memory or reuse the objects allocated, where in a sense, not too many objects become inaccessible or short-lived jobs. There are different opinions when it comes to the usefulness of a no-op garbage collector, but it going to be an interesting addition to Java nonetheless.

- **Dynamic class file constants**: This JEP or JDK enhancement proposal extends the current Java class file format to support a new constant pool form, `CONSTANT_Dynamic`. The idea here is to reduce the cost and disruption of creating new forms of materializable class-file constants.

Apart from the mentioned additions, Java 11 also proposes to remove a couple of modules, such as Java EE and CORBA. These modules were already deprecated in Java 9, and are supposed to be completely removed in Java SDK 11.

Also, Java 11 is supposed to be the **long-term support** (**LTS**) release. This means that, unlike Java 9 and 10, where the JDK support is limited to a few months, Java 11 will be supported for two to three years. Java has decided to release the LTS version every three years, so if we expect Java 11 to be released in September 2018, the next LTS version can be expected in 2021.

Summary

In this chapter, we talked about some important features and best practices in Java. We started our journey from the very beginning of Java releases and touched upon some important milestones for Java. We talked about important Java releases, such as Java 5 and Java 8, which kind of changed the way we code in Java by introducing features such as Generics, Autoboxing, Lambda expressions, Streams, and so on.

Then we got into details about more contemporary releases, that is, Java 9 and Java 10. Java 9 has given us modularization. We can now think of Java code in terms of various modules and choose the ones that are needed for our application. Java 9 also added JShell to its arsenal, which helps us try out and experiment with the language without actually writing and compiling classes. Java 9 added the capability of defining private methods in interfaces. In addition, we also got new features in streams, collections, arrays, and so on with Java 9.

Java 10 gives us the flexibility of declaring variables with the `var` keyword without explicitly mentioning object types. We discussed the limitation of using var and why we need to be careful when using var to declare objects to avoid jeopardizing the readability and maintainability of the code. We also talked about `copyOf` methods to create immutable copies of collections and garbage collection improvements in Java 10.

Finally, we talked about what we can expect in Java 11, such as additions to garbage collection and using var with Lambda. Java 11 is expected to be a long-term release, unlike Java 9 and 10. And, as per the Oracles 3-year policy, the next long-term release should be expected somewhere in 2021, after Java 11.

Java has come a long way since its creation and it keeps on re-inventing itself time and time again. There is a lot more to come in the future, and it will be interesting to view Java's future growth.

Other Books You May Enjoy

If you enjoyed this book, you may be interested in these other books by Packt:

Java 9 Data Structures and Algorithms
Debasish Ray Chawdhuri

ISBN: 978-1-78588-934-9

- Understand the fundamentals of algorithms, data structures, and measurement of complexity
- Find out what general purpose data structures are, including arrays, linked lists, double ended linked lists, and circular lists
- Get a grasp on the basics of abstract data types—stack, queue, and double ended queue
- See how to use recursive functions and immutability while understanding and in terms of recursion
- Handle reactive programming and its related data structures
- Use binary search, sorting, and efficient sorting—quicksort and merge sort
- Work with the important concept of trees and list all nodes of the tree, traversal of tree, search trees, and balanced search trees
- Apply advanced general purpose data structures, priority queue-based sorting, and random access immutable linked lists
- Gain a better understanding of the concept of graphs, directed and undirected graphs, undirected trees, and much more

Java 9 Programming Blueprints

Jason Lee

ISBN: 978-1-78646-019-6

- Learn how to package Java applications as modules by using the Java Platform Module System
- Implement process management in Java by using the all-new process handling API
- Integrate your applications with third-party services in the cloud
- Interact with mail servers using JavaMail to build an application that filters spam messages
- Learn to use JavaFX to build rich GUI based applications, which are an essential element of application development
- Write microservices in Java using platform libraries and third-party frameworks
- Integrate a Java application with MongoDB to build a cloud-based note taking application

Leave a review - let other readers know what you think

Please share your thoughts on this book with others by leaving a review on the site that you bought it from. If you purchased the book from Amazon, please leave us an honest review on this book's Amazon page. This is vital so that other potential readers can see and use your unbiased opinion to make purchasing decisions, we can understand what our customers think about our products, and our authors can see your feedback on the title that they have worked with Packt to create. It will only take a few minutes of your time, but is valuable to other potential customers, our authors, and Packt. Thank you!

Index

A

abstract factory 38
Adapter pattern
  about 78, 127
  examples 79, 82
  implementation 79
  intent 78
Amazon Web Services (AWS) 185
applicability and examples, chain-of-responsibility
    pattern
  event handlers 52
  log handlers 52
  servlets 52
applicability and examples, command pattern
  asynchronous method invocation 55
  composite commands 55
  undo/redo operations 55
application architecture 196
application programming interfaces (API) 174
applicatives 118
aspects-oriented programming (AOP) 199
association
  about 16
  aggregation 16
asynchronous-communication pattern 178, 180
attach method 65
attributes, reactive systems
  elastic 140
  message-driven 140
  resilient 140
  responsive 140
autoscaling pattern 190

B

bounded-queue pattern 184
Bridge pattern
  about 91
  actors 93
  examples 93, 94
  implementation 92
  intent 92
buffer operator 150
builder pattern
  about 40, 126
  anonymous builders, with method chaining 44
  car builder example 41
  simplified builder pattern 43
bulkhead pattern 185

C

caching pattern 180, 182
catch operator 161
chain-of-responsibility pattern
  about 49, 128
  applicability and examples 52
  implementation 50, 51
  intent 50
circuit-breaker pattern 183
class diagram, chain-of-responsibility pattern
  Client 51
  ConcreteHandler 51
  Handler 51
class diagram, command pattern
  Client 54
  ConcreteCommand 54
  Invoker 54
  Receiver 54
class diagram, interpreter pattern
  AbstractExpression 57
  Context 57
  NonTerminalExpression 57
  TerminalExpression 57

class diagram, iterator pattern
  Aggregate 62
  ConcreteAggregate 62
  ConcreteIterator 62
  Iterator 62
class diagram, mediator pattern
  Colleague 66
  ConcreteColleague 66
  ConcreteMediator 66
  Mediator 66
class diagram, memento pattern
  caretaker 68
  memento 68
  originator 68
class diagram, observer pattern
  ConcreteSubject 65
  Observer 65
  Subject 65
class diagram, strategy pattern
  ConcreteStrategy 71
  Context 71
  Strategy 71
class diagram, visitor pattern
  ConcreteElementA and ConcreteElementB 74
  ConcreteVisitor 74
  Element 74
  Visitor 74
class relations, UML
  about 14
  association 16
  dependency 16
  generalization 15
  realization 15
closure 116
Colleague interface 66
combine operator 158
command pattern
  about 53, 128
  applicability and examples 55
  implementation 53
  intent 53
Composite pattern
  about 95
  examples 97
  implementation 96

  intent 95
  composition 115
  ConcreteAggregate 62
  ConcreteElementA 74
  ConcreteIterator 62
  controller 204
  create operator 146
  currying process 116

D

debounce operator 154
declarative programming 10
Decorator pattern
  about 88, 127
  examples 90, 91
  implementation 89
  implementation diagram, actors 90
  intent 89
deep clone 46
defer operator 146
Dependency inversion principle 24
design patterns 17
design principles 17
detach method 65
distinct operator 154
do operator 162
Don't Repeat Yourself (DRY) 120

E

early/eager instantiation 31
elasticity pattern
  about 186
  autoscaling pattern 190
  self-containment pattern 191
  single responsibility pattern 186
  stateless-services pattern 188
elementAt operator 155
empty operator 147
enterprise service bus (ESB) 214
error handling
  about 161
  catch operator, using 161
  do operator, using 162
  retry operator, using 163

using operator, using 163
event-driven communication pattern 191
execute around method
  about 136
  examples 136
  intent 136
extension object 77

F

factory method pattern
  about 36
  anonymous concrete factory 38
  versus abstract factory 40
factory pattern
  about 31
  abstract factory 38
  factory method pattern 36
  factory method, versus abstract factory 40
  simple factory pattern 32
  simple factory pattern, versus factory method 40
fail-fast pattern 182
failure-handling pattern 184
Façade pattern
  about 99
  actors 100
  examples 101, 103
  implementation 100
  intent 99
filter operator 155
first-class functions 114
first/last operator 156
flatMap operator 150
flowable 144
Flyweight pattern
  about 103
  actors 105
  examples 105, 108
  implementation 104
  intent 104
from operator 147
functional design patterns
  about 131
  execute around method 136
  MapReduce 131
  memoization 134

Tail call optimization (TCO) 133
functional programming, in java
  about 119
  lambda expressions 120
  stream creator operations 122
  stream intermediate operations 122
  stream terminal operations 125
  streams 121
functional programming
  about 11, 111
  applicatives 118
  closure 116
  collections, versus streams working 11
  composition 115
  currying process 116
  first-class functions 114
  functors 117
  higher-order functions 115
  immutability 117
  lambda expression 113
  monads 119
  pure function 114
  referential transparency 114
functors 117

G

Gang Of Four (GOF) patterns 18, 77
garbage collection (GC) 250
groupBy operator 152

I

idempotency pattern 193
immutability 117
imperative programming
  about 6
  example 6
Interface Segregation Principle (ISP) 22
interpreter pattern
  about 56, 128
  applicability and examples 60
  implementation 57, 58
  intent 56
interval operator 148
iterator pattern

about 61, 129
applicability and examples 63
implementation 61, 63
intent 61

J

Java 10
  application class data sharing 252
  copyOf method for collections 249
  feature additions 251
  Graal compiler 252
  Local variable type inference 248
  local variable type inference 247
  parallelization of full garbage collection 250
  time-based release monitoring 251
Java 11
  expected features 253
Java 5
  features 230
Java 8
  features 231
Java 9
  additions, to Optional class 243
  enhancements, in streams 240, 241
  feature additions 245, 246
  immutable collections 241
  Java platform module system 232, 235
  JShell 236
  method addition, in arrays 242
  new HTTP client 244
  private methods, in interfaces 239
Java programming
  paradigms 6
Java Runtime Environment (JRE) 3, 232
Java Virtual Machine (JVM) 230
Java
  features 229
  history 229
  supported versions 232
javax.servlet.Filter
  reference link 52
join operator 159
JShell
  about 236
  installation 143

JSON Web Token (JWT) 189
Just in Time compiler (JIT) 5

L

lambda expression 113
layered architecture
  about 196
  benefits 203
  Business layer 198
  challenges 203
  Controller/web service layer 198
  Data access layer 199
  example 199, 201, 202
  Presentation layer 198
  Service layer 198
  tiers, versus layers 203
Liskov Substitution Principle (LSP) 21, 22
List Programming (LISP) 111
load pattern
  about 132
  examples 133
  intent 132

M

map operator 153
MapReduce
  about 131
  examples 131
  intent 131
  load pattern 132
marker interface 77
maven
  reference 142
mediator pattern
  about 65, 66
  applicability and examples 67
  implementation 66
  intent 66
memento pattern
  about 67
  applicability 69
  implementation 67
  intent 67
memoization

about 134
examples 135
intent 134
merge operator 160
message-driven implementation patterns
about 191
event-driven communication pattern 191
idempotency pattern 193
publisher-subscriber pattern 192
microservice architecture
about 217
benefits 219
challenges 220
communication 219
example 217, 218
model 204
Model View Controller architecture
about 204
benefits 210
challenges 211
contemporary MVC implementation 210
controller 204
example 207, 208
model 204
view 204
module 77
monads
about 119
reference link 119
monitoring patterns 185

N

null object pattern
about 72
implementation 73

O

object pool pattern 46
object relational mapping (ORM) framework 199
object-oriented paradigm
about 7
abstraction 8
encapsulation 7
inheritance 8

object and classes 7
polymorphism 9
Observable, filtering
about 154
debounce operator, using 154
distinct operator, using 154
elementAt operator, using 155
filter operator, using 155
first/last operator, using 156
sample operator, using 156
skip operator, using 157
take operator, using 157
Observables, combining
combine operator, using 158
join operator, using 159
merge operator, using 160
zip operator, using 160
Observables, creating
create operator, using 146
defer operator, using 146
empty operator, using 147
from operator, using 147
interval operator, using 148
range operator, using 148
repeat operator, using 149
timer operator, using 148
Observables, transforming
buffer operator, using 150
flatMap operator, using 152
groupBy operator, using 152
map operator, using 153
scan operator, using 153
subscribe operator, using 149
window operator, using 153
Observables
about 144
cold 145
combining 158
creating 145
filtering 154
hot 145
transforming 149
observer pattern
about 64, 129
implementation 64

intent 64
observers 144
OOP design patterns
  adapter 127
  builder 126
  chain of responsibility 128
  command 128
  decorator 127
  interpreter 128
  iterator 129
  observer 129
  reimplementing 125
  singleton 125
  strategy 130
  template method 130
Open/closed principle 20

P

Plain Old Java Object (POJO) 176
prototype pattern
  about 45
  shallow clone, versus deep clone 46
Proxy pattern
  about 84
  cache proxy 84
  examples 86, 88
  implementation 85
  intent 85
  protection proxy 84
  remote proxy 84
  Virtual and smart proxies. 84
publisher-subscriber pattern 192
pure function 114

Q

quickest-reply pattern 182

R

range operator 148
reactive programming 139, 141
referential transparency 114
repeat operator 149
Representational State Transfer (REST)
  about 174

versus SOAP 213
request-response pattern 171, 174, 177
resilience patterns
  about 183
  bounded-queue pattern 184
  bulkhead pattern 185
  circuit-breaker pattern 183
  failure-handling pattern 184
  monitoring patterns 185
responsiveness patterns
  about 171
  asynchronous-communication pattern 178
  caching pattern 180
  fail-fast pattern 182
  fan-out pattern 182
  quickest-reply pattern 182
  request-response pattern 171
retry operator 163
RxJava framework
  installing 142
  JShell installation 143
  Maven installation 142
RxJava
  about 141
  example project 166

S

sample operator 156
scan operator 153
schedulers 164, 166
self-containment pattern 191
serverless architecture
  about 220
  benefits 227
  challenges 228
  example 221, 222, 223, 225
  independence, from infrastructure planning 227
service-oriented architecture (SOA)
  about 211
  benefits 216
  challenges 216
  components 213
  enterprise service bus (ESB) 214
  example 212, 213
  web services 213

shallow clone
  versus deep clone 46
simple factory pattern
  about 32
  simple factory pattern, with class registration
    using Product.newInstance 35
  simple factory pattern, with registration using
    reflection 34
  static factory 33
  versus factory method 40
single responsibility pattern 18, 186
singleton pattern
  about 27, 125
  early loading 31
  lazy loading 31
  lock-free thread-safe singleton 30
  synchronized singleton, with double-checking
    locking mechanism 30
  synchronized singletons 29
skip operator 157
Smalltalk 5
SOAP
  versus REST 213
SOLID
  Dependency inversion principle 24
  Interface Segregation Principle (ISP) 22
  Liskov Substitution Principle (LSP) 20
  open/closed principle 20
  single responsibility pattern 18
state pattern 70
stateless-services pattern 188
strategy pattern
  about 70, 130
  implementation 71
  intent 70
stream creator operations 122
stream intermediate operations 122
stream terminal operations 125
streams 121
subjects 166
subscribe operator 149
subscriptions 144
synchronized singleton

about 29
  with double-checked locking mechanism 30

T

Tail call optimization (TCO)
  about 133
  examples 134
  intent 133
take operator 157
template method pattern
  about 71, 130
  implementation 72
  intent 72
The Reactive Manifesto
  reference 139
timer operator 148
twin 78

U

Unified Modeling Language (UML)
  about 12, 14
  behavior diagrams 13
  class relations 14
  structural diagrams 13
update 65
using operator 163

V

view 204
visitor pattern
  about 73, 74
  implementation 74
  intent 74

W

window operator 153

Z

zip operator 160

Λ

λ Calculus Interpreter
  reference link 113

www.ingramcontent.com/pod-product-compliance
Lightning Source LLC
Chambersburg PA
CBHW080631060326
40690CB00021B/4895